Fodor's InFo

TURKS
ISLANDS

14
TOP EXPERIENCES

The Turks and Caicos offer terrific experiences that should be on every traveler's list. Here are Fodor's top picks for a memorable trip.

1 Grace Bay

One of the world's best beaches, Grace Bay has 12 miles of powdery white sand that frame a calm stretch of turquoise sea. Despite its popularity, you're sure to find some solitude. *(Ch. 2)*

2 Coco Bistro

This elegant Providenciales restaurant is popular with vacationers and locals alike for its French- and West Indies–inspired cuisine. *(Ch. 2)*

3 Stand-up Paddleboarding

The latest rage on Providenciales is the perfect way to explore the island's lush mangroves. You can also rent a board on Grace Bay. *(Ch. 2)*

4 Grand Turk

The atmospheric capital of the Turks and Caicos brims with old Caribbean charm and has beautiful beaches protected by magnificent reefs. *(Ch. 4)*

5 Quinton Dean

Celebrated local musician Quinton Dean performs at different venues around Providenciales—when he's not off touring with Prince. Catch a performance if you can. *(Ch. 2)*

6 Scuba Diving

Long before luxury resorts attracted beach-goers, divers came to the Turks and Caicos for superb reefs along the Columbus Passage. *(Ch. 4)*

7 Sunsets

Gorgeous sunsets can be experienced all over, but the poolside view from Amanyara, a Fodor's Choice resort on Providenciales' far west end, is especially spectacular. *(Ch. 2)*

8 Family Fun

Shallow waters, fine sand, and loads of kid-friendly activities make Providenciales one of the Caribbean's best family destinations. *(Ch. 2)*

9 Local Color

To see real island culture, go where the locals go: Bugaloo's in Five Cays. Here, you can feast on conch with your feet in the sand and hear live music on Sundays. *(Ch. 2)*

10 Half Moon Bay

Accessible only by boat, this natural sandbar rivals Grace Bay for beauty. Go with Caicos Dream Tours for a truly memorable experience. *(Ch. 2)*

11 Stingray Encounter

Wade into the shallow waters around Gibbs Cay, a small uninhabited islet off Grand Turk, to swim with stingrays in a natural environment. *(Ch. 4)*

12 Whale-watching

From January through April, humpback whales pass so close to Salt Cay that you can see them from the beach. On some days, you can even snorkel with them. *(Ch. 5)*

13 Spas

The spas in the Turks and Caicos are some of the Caribbean's finest. Many feature invigorating local conch scrubs and relaxing open-air massages. *(Ch. 2)*

14 Luxury Resorts

Providenciales has many luxury resorts, like the gorgeous Seven Stars. Even if you don't stay here, be sure to splurge on sundowner drinks on The Deck. *(Ch. 2)*

CONTENTS

ABOUT THIS GUIDE

Fodor's Recommendations

Everything in this guide is worth doing—we don't cover what isn't—but exceptional sights, hotels, and restaurants are recognized with additional accolades. Fodor'sChoice★ indicates our top recommendations. Care to nominate a new place? Visit Fodors.com/contact-us.

Trip Costs

We list prices wherever possible to help you budget well. Hotel and restaurant price categories from **$** to **$$$$** are noted alongside each recommendation. For hotels, we include the lowest cost of a standard double room in high season. For restaurants, we cite the average price of a main course at dinner or, if dinner isn't served, at lunch. For attractions, we always list adult admission fees; discounts are usually available for children, students, and senior citizens.

Hotels

Our local writers vet every hotel to recommend the best overnights in each price category, from budget to expensive. Unless otherwise specified, you can expect private bath, phone, and TV in your room. For expanded hotel reviews, facilities, and deals, visit Fodors.com.

Restaurants

Unless we state otherwise, restaurants are open for lunch and dinner daily. We mention dress code only when there's a specific requirement and reservations only when they're essential or not accepted. To make restaurant reservations, visit Fodors.com.

Credit Cards

The hotels and restaurants in this guide typically accept credit cards. If not, we'll say so.

Top Picks

★ Fodor'sChoice

Listings

⊠ Address
⊠ Branch address
🕰 Mailing address
☎ Telephone
🖷 Fax
🌐 Website
✎ E-mail

🖃 Admission fee
🕓 Open/closed times
Ⓜ Subway
✛ Directions or Map coordinates

Hotels & Restaurants

🏨 Hotel
🛏 Number of rooms
🍽 Meal plans

✕ Restaurant
🍸 Reservations
🏛 Dress code
🚫 No credit cards
$ Price

Other

⇨ See also
☞ Take note
🏌 Golf facilities

EXPERIENCE THE TURKS AND CAICOS

WELCOME TO
THE TURKS AND CAICOS

The Turks and Caicos are made up of more than 40 islands cast upon breathtakingly beautiful cerulean waters. Although white, soft-sand beaches and calm, warm waters are shared among all the islands, their landscapes vary. The flatter, more arid islands of Grand Turk, Salt Cay, South Caicos, Pine Cay, and Providenciales are covered with low-lying bush and scrub, whereas the islands of Middle Caicos, North Caicos, and Parrot Cay are greener, with more undulating landscapes. In addition to these eight inhabited islands, there are the many smaller cays and uninhabited East Caicos that help make up this southern tip of the Lucayan Archipelago, just 575 miles (862 km) southeast of Miami on the third-largest coral reef system in the world.

Discovery

Although the first recorded sighting of the Turks and Caicos Islands was in 1512, there is a much-disputed possibility suggesting that Columbus first made landfall on Grand Turk on his voyage to the New World in 1492. Today this delightful string of islands has become an exclusive and highly prized destination, perhaps because of their history of anonymity.

Changing Hands

The Turks and Caicos Islands were controlled by France and Spain in the past, and then indirectly through Bermuda, the Bahamas, and finally Jamaica before becoming a separate autonomous British Overseas Territory with its own governor in 1973. These islands were initially desirable because of their salt production. In fact, there was a time when Salt Cay provided much of the salt that supplied the whole of United States and Canada.

Reefs and Wrecks

It's estimated that some 1,000 shipwrecks surround the islands. Some island residents may be descendants of those shipwrecked off the Spanish slave ship *Trouvadore,* which ran aground off East Caicos in 1841. But the most famous wreck is probably that of the Spanish galleon *Nuestra Senora de la Concepcion,* which sank after hitting a shallow reef in 1641 in the Silver Shoals, between the Turks and Caicos and Hispaniola. William Phips had recovered a small portion of the treasure by 1687. However, Burt Webber discovered the majority of it in 1978. The wreck contained treasure worth millions, as well as priceless artifacts, including Chinese porcelain from the late Ming period.

Tumultuous Times

Two female pirates, Anne Bonny and Mary Read, captured a Spanish treasure ship in 1718, then settled on Pirate Cay, which is now known as Parrot Cay. Only two years later a pirate named Francoise L'Olonnois moved onto French Cay, using it as a base from which to raid passing ships. Many say that his treasure is still buried there on the edge of the Caicos Banks. On the south shore of Providenciales carvings can be found among the rocks, supposedly maps to buried treasures.

The People

Only 31,500 people live in the Turks and Caicos Islands. Less than half are "Belongers," the term for the native population. All are descendants of loyalist slaves, brought south after the American Declaration of Independence drove the loyalists to seek another haven in which to grow their cotton and sugarcane. The ancestors of those from Grand Turk, Salt Cay, and South Caicos worked in the salt industry, descended mostly from Bermudian slaves who settled here in the 1600s. Nowadays the majority of residents work in tourism, fishing, and offshore finance.

The Rise of Providenciales

The political and historical capital of the country is Grand Turk, with the seat of government there. Most of the tourism development, however, is on Providenciales, more commonly known as "Provo." Thanks to the beauty of its north shore, visitors may enjoy the miles of ivory sand that stretch along its graceful curve; Grace Bay is consistently rated as the best beach in the world. Provo has become a hub of activity since the 1990s, as resorts, spas, and restaurants have been built and the resident population has grown to some 15,000. It is also the temporary home for the vast majority of visitors who come to the Turks and Caicos Islands.

Remnants of History

Marks of the country's colonial past can be found in the wood-and-stone Bermudian-style clapboard houses that line the streets on Grand Turk, Salt Cay, and South Caicos. Throughout the Caicos Islands, visitors may explore the ruins of several loyalist plantations now protected by the Turks & Caicos National Trust; slave quarters, a great house, stone pens, wells, and cauldrons all draw us back in time to feel what lives were like for those growing cotton and sisal in these islands. Much of this history is also recounted in the Turks and Caicos National Museum on Grand Turk.

WHAT'S WHERE

1 Providenciales. Provo has most of the accommodations in the Turks and Caicos and gets the majority of visitors. Come if you are seeking miles of soft sand, luxurious accommodations, crystal-clear water, and fine dining. But don't come for nightlife—there are only a few hot spots that will keep you out all night.

2 The Caicos and the Cays. Although most of the cays are uninhabited, there is the ultraluxurious private-island resort of Parrot Cay, as well as the laid-back tranquillity to be experienced at the Meridian Club on the private island of Pine Cay. South Caicos is all about diving and snorkeling, fishing and exploring; on North and Middle Caicos, days can be spent simply beachcombing and sunbathing.

3 Grand Turk. The historic capital of the Turks and Caicos gets many more visitors by cruise ship than as overnight guests. Come here if you like to dive or just relax, and if you're on a budget, you'll find that most prices are more reasonable than those on Provo.

4 Salt Cay. Step off the ferry or plane here, and you may feel as if you've landed in 1950. Come to relax on one of the prettiest beaches in all the Turks and Caicos or go diving. In season you may want to whale watch. Don't come expecting more than rustic accommodations and basic service.

TO BAHAMA

Caicos Passage

Three Mary's Ce
Parrot Cay
Fort George Cay
Football Fields
Northwest   Little/Big Water Cay   Pine Ca
Point
Providenciales   Caic
Cheshire Hall   Grace Bay   Conc
Sapodilla Hill   Farm
Southwest   Juba Point
Bluff

West
Caicos   C   A   I   C   O

Southwest   C
Reef
Molasses Reef   CAICOS

BANK

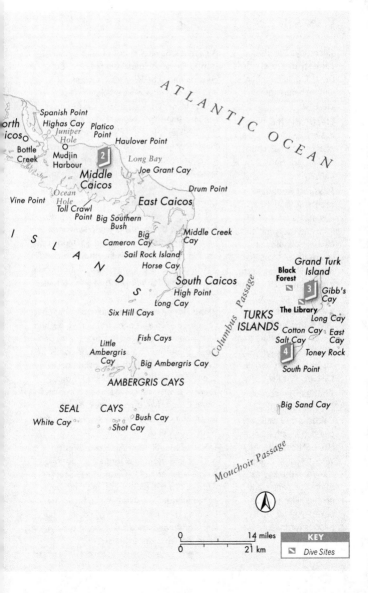

ATLANTIC OCEAN

Spanish Point
Highas Cay
Juniper Hole
Platico Point
Haulover Point

orth icos

Bottle Creek

Mudjin Harbour

2

Long Bay
Joe Grant Cay

Middle Caicos

Ocean Hole

Vine Point

Toll Crawl Point

Big Southern Bush

East Caicos

Drum Point

Big Cameron Cay

Middle Creek Cay

Sail Rock Island

Horse Cay

ISLANDS

South Caicos

High Point

Long Cay

Six Hill Cays

Grand Turk Island

Black Forest

3

Gibb's Cay

The Library

Long Cay

TURKS ISLANDS

Cotton Cay

Salt Cay

East Cay

4

Toney Rock

South Point

Columbus Passage

Little Ambergris Cay

Fish Cays

Big Ambergris Cay

AMBERGRIS CAYS

SEAL CAYS

White Cay

Bush Cay

Shot Cay

Big Sand Cay

Mouchoir Passage

0 — 14 miles
0 — 21 km

KEY
◪ Dive Sites

TURKS AND CAICOS PLANNER

Essentials

Currency: The official currency of the islands is the U.S. dollar. All banks will exchange foreign currency.

Electricity: The current is suitable for all U.S. appliances, and electrical sockets are North American–style.

Passport Requirements: A valid passport is required for all visitors, and everyone must have an ongoing or return ticket. Visas are not necessary for North Americans or EU citizens. Be sure to check with your consulate to see if one is needed for your travel; most visitors transit through the United States, where clearing customs is a necessity.

Phones: The country code for the Turks and Caicos is 649; calls are charged as international. U.S. GSM cell phones work throughout the islands, but many car-rental companies and private villas provide pay-as-you-go loaner phones for free.

Getting Here and Around

Air Travel: Several major airlines fly non-stop to Providenciales from the U.S., but carriers and schedules vary seasonally. You can fly nonstop from Atlanta (Delta), Dallas (American), Charlotte (USAirways), Miami (American), New York–JFK (Delta and JetBlue), Newark–EWR (United), and Philadelphia (USAirways). Once on Provo, InterCaribbean and Caicos Express Airways fly to North Caicos, South Caicos, Grand Turk, and Salt Cay.

Car Rentals: You can get by on Provo without a car, especially if you are staying on Grace Bay, but rentals are relatively inexpensive, ranging from around $50/day and up. On the other islands they hover around $100/day. Gas is expensive and most often must be paid for in cash. And don't forget that driving is on the left, British-style!

Island Hopping: You can make air connections to four other islands from Provo (Grand Turk, South Caicos, North Caicos, and Salt Cay). There are also several ferries daily between Provo and North Caicos; a causeway connects North Caicos to Middle Caicos. There is a ferry service between Provo and South Caicos two days a week. You can reach Salt Cay by ferry—but only when the weather is good.

Taxis: Taxis will be at the Provo airport, but it is important to arrange transportation before your arrival in Grand Turk, South Caicos, North Caicos, and Salt Cay; your accommodation will assist you. If you are heading over just for the day, contact your lunch destination and ask them to assist you. Note that taxis are expensive.

1

Accommodations

Most of the accommodation along Providenciales's Grace Bay is condo-style, with extra space for families and fully equipped kitchens and laundry facilities. However, you will also find a few hotel room–style resorts to choose from. The majority of places to stay on the outer islands are small inns. What you give up in luxury, however, you gain back tenfold in island charm.

Another alternative to a resort-style vacation is staying in one of the numerous villas that dot the islands. On Provo you will find a large selection, from one-bedroom cottages perfect for a honeymoon to villas that sleep more than 20 people, ideal for that extended-family holiday. On the less busy outer islands your options are limited. With demand high, especially in the busy season, it makes sense to plan as far ahead as possible. Those with flexibility can take advantage of the off-season.

There are also two very private ultraluxury resorts to choose from at this time: Parrot Cay and Amanyara.

Saving Money

Although the Turks and Caicos are a fairly expensive vacation destination, there are ways to save. Many resorts offer free nights and extra perks during the off-season. Rates are lower a block or two from the beach. Be sure to check if the hotel is part of a package deal, rolling airfare and accommodation into one. Turksandcaicosreservations. com is a good place to start. Staying in condo-style accommodation or a villa means you can cook some meals yourself. Note that airlines will accept a cooler of food as long as perishables are frozen and vacuum-sealed; customs will allow it to enter.

Visitor Information

You can get information from the Turks & Caicos Islands Tourist Board (⊕ *www.turksandcaicos tourism.com*). Tourist offices on Providenciales and Grand Turk are open daily from 9 to 5. Visitors should also check out ⊕ *www.wherewhenhow. com*, a terrific source with links to every place to stay, plus all the restaurants, excursions, and transportation on Providenciales (and to a lesser degree the other islands).

Weddings

The residency requirement is 24 hours, after which you can apply for a marriage license at the registrar in Grand Turk. You must present a passport, birth certificate, and proof of current marital status. The current fee is $50. Using a local planner will be helpful. Many resorts now have their own in-house service. Or, you may try the most experienced local company, Nila Destinations (⊕ *www.niladestinations. com*).

IF YOU LIKE

The Best Beaches in the World

Most people come to Turks and Caicos for the beautiful beaches—miles of white coral sand and crystal-clear waters that surround each of the islands that make up this archipelago.

Visitors and residents alike all have their favorite stretch of sand. Most people come to Turks and Caicos to enjoy Providenciales's Grace Bay. It is the best of all worlds: miles of uninterrupted brilliant blue against a backdrop of white-tipped waves, with its powder-fine sand that stays cool to the touch even in the heat of the day. If you wish to break away from the buzz of Grace Bay, there are many other exquisite beaches right on Provo. Taylor Bay and Sapodilla Beach are wonderful small crescents with shallow waters that are perfect for small children. Long Bay is dotted with private villas, perfect for quiet beach walks and collecting naturally tossed conch shells. Half Moon Bay on Little Water Cay and Fort George Cay's shoreline are a photographer's delight, even though they now attract many visitors. Pine Cay and Big Water Cay may have the best stretches of uninterrupted sand. Mudjin Harbour on Middle Caicos is the most dramatic, winged on one side by towering cliffs and isolated coves. And then there are those who claim that the most beautiful beach of all is North Beach on Salt Cay.

The Best Fishing

For those on the Turks and Caicos to simply relax, taking a dip in the turquoise waters can't be beat. But for others who like a bit of adventure, one of the best ways to experience these islands is to take a fishing excursion. Try deep-sea, bone-, or bottom-fishing, with a bonus of seeing areas that are otherwise unreachable without a boat.

The beauty of bonefishing is that you don't have to go out in the deep waters, so it is something the whole family may enjoy. If you're a fly fisher, you can try your luck by walking into Flamingo or Turtle lakes on the south side of Provo or hire a skiff to take you into the waters between Provo and Middle Caicos. South Caicos also has excellent bonefishing.

Deep-sea fishing takes you outside the reef into the deep waters that surround these islands. It is not quite as hard-core as one might imagine; there are well-stocked refrigerators providing cold drinks throughout the day, rotating cushioned chairs for the "big fight," and a fish finder to aid in the hunt. The ship's mate baits multiple lines with or without your help, and the lines are lowered from the tower.

Reef fishing is another alternative. The experience involves a quiet afternoon of contemplation. You are after grouper, snapper, triggerfish, or sturgeon while anchoring in a channel or out near the reef. It is a casting sport, with the fish taking the line to wait out your patience under a coral head.

Excellent Diving

With the third-largest barrier reef in the world, dramatic walls that ultimately drop to 6,000 feet, and consistently sunny days on top of crystal-clear, calm waters, the Turks and Caicos are a diver's dream destination. The visibility is unfailingly some of the best in the world, averaging 100 to 200 feet on most days. There is a wide variety of marine life with an unending number of dive sites to explore, placing it on the map as one of the top dive destinations in the world.

Each island offers something unique in the way of diving. In Providenciales there are dive sites just over the reef in Grace Bay for those who want to keep it "close to home," but all dive operators also venture farther afield: Provo's calm Northwest Point and nearby West Caicos with its superb wall, and pristine and protected French Cay, on the edge of the Caicos Banks. Grand Turk has dramatic walls close to shore. Reefs off Salt Cay have not seen many divers, so you will have them virtually all to yourself. Salt Cay is also the jumping-off point for divers to explore the wreck of the *Endymion,* a sailing vessel that met its demise in 1790. Although South Caicos also offers unspoiled reef to explore with exceptional visibility, note that there are no longer any dive companies operating locally. Big Blue Unlimited out of Provo, however, offers charter services. Expect to see sharks, dolphins, rays, turtles, and eels, as well as myriad other marine life.

Great Snorkeling

Many visitors return year after year because of the exceptional opportunities to snorkel in the Turks and Caicos. The waters are protected by the barrier reef just offshore and are therefore calm, providing relatively relaxing spots in which to snorkel in patch coral close to shore. Within Grace Bay on Providenciales, the Bight Reef is a favorite for many, as Grace Bay guests may access it easily in front of Coral Gardens Resort. Farther along is Smith's Reef at the entrance to Turtle Cove. Although the snorkeling is excellent, the waters here are a little rougher, and there's no buoyed area, so you'll need to be careful of boat traffic. On the other side of the entrance you'll find Babalua Reef, a drive away from Grace Bay. This reef is farther offshore, but for a good swimmer, the experience is a little less busy.

Alternatively, you may wish to take a half- or full-day snorkeling excursion to one of the many uninhabited cays and secluded coves, or out to the main reef itself. There are many companies to choose from, all of which provide a great customized experience. You may want to dive for conch, snorkel for sand dollars, or stop to find submerged cannons left from yesteryear. Most visitors wish to stop at Little Water Cay (otherwise known as Iguana Island) to see the rock iguanas, and everyone wants to make at least a brief stop on one of the cays to experience a quiet, secluded beach.

If you want a more private experience, have a boat drop you off on one of the many secluded beaches for the day, leaving you with a cooler full of food and drink, along with beach chairs, umbrellas, and snorkel gear. There you can snorkel directly from the beach, and you'll often be alone.

A New Island Every Day

With eight inhabited islands, you can visit a different island every day of your weeklong stay in the Turks and Caicos. From Provo's Walkin Marina at Heaving Down Rock, you can take one of several daily ferries over to North Caicos, rent a car, and explore plantation ruins, Cottage Pond, and resident flamin-

gos, then drive over the causeway to Middle Caicos to visit limestone caves or hike the Crossing Place Trail. You will also want to enjoy the beauty of Mudjin Harbour or another secluded beach. There is also a much longer ferry that goes over to South Caicos twice a week. Alternatively, there are daily flights to South Caicos via InterCaribbean Airways and Caicos Express Airways.

One of the best day trips is to Grand Turk, with its laid-back charm. Both local airlines offer early-morning 30-minute flights that return the same day. Stroll down Front Street to see its original clapboard buildings dating back to the 1600s and stop at the beautiful Anglican Church. The Turks and Caicos National Museum has exhibits that include those on John Glenn's first touchdown off of Grand Turk, the Molasses Reef wreck, local bush medicine, and the early inhabitants of the islands. There's also a lighthouse at the tip of the island and the original prison to visit. You can also swim with the stingrays through an excursion to Gibbs Cay. Stop at the Sand Bar on the way back to the airport for a drink on the deck overlooking the water. Give yourself two days on the island and you can even hop over to Salt Cay, referred to as "the island that time forgot."

WHEN TO GO

Peak season in the Turks and Caicos runs from American Thanksgiving through mid-April, when prices average 20% to 50% higher than in the summer. July and August are becoming more and more popular, however, with North Americans not wanting to chance a rainy summer vacation closer to home. Here the summers are guaranteed hot, with only midday rain showers once in a while.

Climate

Daytime temperatures in the Turks and Caicos Islands range from 75°F to 85°F year-round, except during the hottest months of August and September, when temperatures jump into the 90s and above. Evening temperatures can sometimes dip to 50°F. The islands are among the driest in the Caribbean region, with an average of 350 days of sunshine, light trade winds, and less humidity than on surrounding islands. Water temperatures range from the high 70s in the winter to the low 80s in the summer. Hurricane season runs from June through November, but very few storms pass through until late August.

Festivals and Events

Most months have an annual event; check *enews.tc* or the Turks & Caicos Tourist Board for actual dates and contact numbers.

January: The Winter Wahoo Fishing Tournament is held at Turtle Cove.

March: Paddy's Pub Crawl is always held on St. Patrick's Day. The Fishing Fools Wahoo open tournament is held in late March, as is The Wine Cellar's Annual Golf and Fishing Tournament. The Rake n' Scrape festival held on North Caicos is a fantastic event for music lovers.

April: The Easter Monday Kite Flying Competition is held on Providenciales the day after Easter.

May: The South Caicos Regatta is held during the last weekend in May. Cinco de Mayo is celebrated along the docks of Turtle Cove on May 5.

October: Annual Halloween parties abound around the islands; visitors can find something for their children to participate in, as well as a festive party for themselves.

December: The Maskanoo Street party and parade is held on Boxing Day (December 26) on Grace Bay Road in Provo. This is a must-see post-Christmas celebration, along with the Junkanoo New Year's Eve street party hosting live bands, parades, and fireworks.

GEOGRAPHY, FLORA, AND FAUNA

The landscape in the Turks and Caicos is relatively flat. In fact, the highest point of land is Flamingo Hill on uninhabited East Caicos at 157 feet. It is also quite dry; the chain experiences the least amount of rainfall of any island nation in the Caribbean region. The beautiful beaches that encircle the islands are made up of coral stone, crushed and ground into sand as soft as powder as it makes its way over the reef into the quieter, more protected waters. Its pearly white appearance creates a stunning contrast to the indescribable hues of the water.

Birds

French Cay is a bird-watcher's dream, protected as a national park. Here you can see dozens of white-cheeked pintail, reddish egrets, and ospreys. The country's national bird, the osprey, can be seen on all the islands, but osprey nests are easier to see at Three Mary Cays on North Caicos or at Splitting Rock on Provo. Bright pink flamingos can be spotted on some islands, especially at Flamingo Pond on North Caicos, the pond on West Caicos, and at Provo's only golf course.

Flora

The official national plant is the Turk's head cactus, so named because of its shape. The best place to see fields of them is on Amber-

gris Cay. Silver palms grow naturally in the scrub, adding a tropical flair to beaches such as Half Moon Bay, but the trees are most numerous on West Caicos. North Caicos is considered the "garden" island, as it receives the most rainfall of the islands and is greener as a result. The cays all have small limestone cliffs that have formed from years of ocean waves.

Other Fauna

Huge blue land crabs come out in the spring after rains. You're more likely to spot one on the sparsely populated islands of North and Middle Caicos, although they can be seen on Provo, too. The queen conchs that thrive in the flats between Provo and Little Water Cay are an important part of the islands' economies. The Turks and Caicos have the largest population of conch in the world, and conch is the most important food on these islands. Conch diving and deep-sea fishing both require fishing permits. The most important indigenous species of the Turks and Caicos is the rock iguana. They're mostly found at Little Water Cay, which is also known as Iguana Island. So beloved are these iguanas that Little Water Cay has been declared a national park. Excursion companies will make a stop to view them.

WHAT'S NEW

The Shore Club will bring life to the secluded Long Bay Beach, a property being developed by the popular Hartling Group of Regent Palms and the Sands Resort. With only 38 suites, it will also have three pools and a spa. Guests will have Long Bay Beach mostly to themselves, because there are no other beachfront properties there. Although much of the resort will be completed by Christmas 2015, the resort is set to open in June 2016.

The biggest changes in the near future will be in South Caicos. Vacationers hardly venture there because it has so little tourism infrastructure. Sailrock, however, is changing all that. It has completed several private rentals, to be offered as private, quiet getaways overlooking the deep blues of the Turks Island Passage. The resort has been coined as "barefoot luxury" with miles of nature trails within preserved wildlife habitats—a perfect spot for those interested in getting away from it all without scrimping on the creature comforts. It is simply stunning in an understated way, and you'll be able to enjoy total privacy or take advantage of the resort facilities in a central location. Sailrock has also developed relationships with companies they know will honor this pristine ecosystem; Big Blue Unlimited offers dive excursions now on South Caicos, along with rental bikes to explore this small island quietly. J&V Tours covers fishing excursions and beach drop-off where you can experience virgin white-sand beaches in total seclusion. (Note that although the brand-new East Bay Resort has been completely finished for several months, no date has been confirmed for the opening of its doors.)

The government has most recently signed a development agreement with Desarrolos Hotel Group, with the groundbreaking of its newest Ritz Carlton slated for as soon as November 2015, just to the west of Seven Stars on Grace Bay.

Those looking for a quieter alternative to Grace Bay will be excited by the prospect of a second luxury hotel and spa nestled amidst the tranquillity of the south side of the island. Viceroy has been granted permission to begin development of a low-density luxury hotel in the Cooper Jack area overlooking the Caicos Banks. With three marinas in the area, the resort is anticipated to have a slightly different vibe.

Murmurings have also included the development of a 41-acre luxury resort on the much quieter Middle Caicos. Aniyana Grand Caicos will be a low-density eco-sensitive boutique hotel, including both beach and lagoon front accommodation set within its very own nature preserve.

KIDS AND FAMILIES

Most family-friendly activities are on Provo, but the rest of the islands—especially Grand Turk—provide plenty of other options.

Accommodations

Most of the accommodations on Provo and the rest of the Turks and Caicos are in condo-style resorts or private rental villas. These are ideal for families because they offer more space, laundry facilities, and full kitchens for cooking meals in. Babysitters can also be arranged to look after young ones while parents enjoy evenings out.

In Provo

At the **Caicos Conch Farm** kids learn about the biggest export from the Turks and Caicos Islands. **Coral Gardens** is great for off-the-beach snorkeling; kids can see colorful fish in waist-deep water. Those eight years of age or older can try Snuba, a surface-supplied diving experience. Without getting wet, little ones may experience the underwater world by climbing on board the Undersea Explorer, a semisubmarine that is even regularly visited by a resident mermaid! On dry land The Bight's **public playground** has swing sets and slides, along with bathrooms. There are **banana boat rides and parasailing, minigolf,** and horseback riding. But a sure thing for families is to contact SURFside Ocean Academy, an outdoor adventure company and licensed school specializing in kids' camps, eco-adventures, and water sports.

Big Blue Unlimited is the most comprehensive water-sports and eco-tour outfit in the Turks and Caicos Islands, specializing in stand-up paddleboarding, kayaking, kiteboarding, snorkel tours, diving, and more.

Outer Islands

On Middle Caicos families can visit one of the largest limestone cave systems in the Caribbean, with its several species of resident bats. **Mudjin Harbour** and Blue Horizon Resort offer hiking trails along the cliffs that are part of the Crossing Place Trail. Within the trail system is a hidden staircase leading to a "secret" beach.

North Caicos has the best plantation ruins to be explored. Wades Green still has remains of the main house, slave quarters, gardens, and rock walls, as well as old cauldrons.

The **Turks and Caicos National Museum can be found on Grand Turk. Gibbs Cay** is always a favorite of kids, offering them a chance to play and to hold gentle stingrays on a secluded "Gilligan's Island." Horseback riding is also a possibility on Grand Turk.

PROVIDENCIALES

By Laura
Adzich-
Brander

PASSENGERS TYPICALLY BECOME SILENT when their plane starts its descent into the Providenciales airport (PLS), mesmerized by the shallow, crystal-clear, turquoise waters of Chalk Sound National Park below. Provo, as most visitors call it, is the most developed part of the island chain. Most of the modern resorts, exquisite spas, water-sports operators, shops, business plazas, restaurants, bars, cafés, and its only golf course are on or close by the prized, 12-mile (18-km) north shore with its exquisite Grace Bay. Despite of the ever-increasing number of taller and grander condominium resorts, it's still possible to find deserted stretches on this priceless, sugar-soft shoreline. When residents begin to groan during the busy season, exclaiming how many people are bustling around, tourists exclaim, "You've got to be kidding. There's no one here!" But for guaranteed seclusion, one can head off to explore the southern shores and western tip of the island or set sail for a private island getaway on one of the many deserted cays nearby. For many, renting a private villa in one of the less developed areas of the island creates the perfect balance.

Providenciales is where the majority of tourists are headed when they come to the Turks and Caicos Islands, or TCI. In fact, regardless of which other island you may be going to, you'll stop here first, as Provo has this country's main international airport, taking in all scheduled international flights. However, with all its modern amenities and unsurpassed beauty there comes a fairly high price tag attached. This is not the island for the budget-conscious traveler to visit; accommodations and dining here are expensive. Provo is definitely an upscale destination. And with this designation, you won't be hassled by beach vendors, and you won't be surrounded by poverty. This is a place to destress and unwind in the loveliest of ways.

Of course, for those with a passion for experiencing the real side of Turks and Caicos, Providenciales is conveniently connected to its family islands through a superb ferry service or several small plane flights a day. There are also myriad boat charters that can get you off the island and back again—in a flash. You can head out in the morning and be back to enjoy dinner in one of the many fabulous restaurants islandwide, followed by the comforts of your five-star hotel. No roughing it unless you wish to, and the sky's the limit. Enjoy!

PLANNING

GETTING HERE AND AROUND

AIR TRAVEL

All international flights arrive in Providenciales (PLS); from here there are regularly scheduled flights to Grand Turk, Salt Cay, and South Caicos. Charter flights can also get you into North Caicos. Both InterCaribbean and Caicos Express Airways offer regularly scheduled flights and a private charter service.

In the past two years the airport in Providenciales has gone through a considerable upgrade, and it now does a much better job of handling the large number of departures on busy weekends. However, it is recommended that if your vacation time is flexible, try booking your flights so that you arrive and depart outside of weekends. Evening arrivals are also preferable, as exiting into the heat and humidity can be a bit daunting for those arriving from colder climates.

There is a very comfortable VIP lounge at the airport through VIP Flyers Club. The cost is $50/person for use of the lounge; expedited travelers take precedence, so availability is pending. For departing guests, expedited services include priority security screening and check-in, and the use of their tranquil 40-person lounge overlooking the runway until flight time. This extends your vacation time, reducing all stress associated with the din of regular departure procedures. Upon arriving in Provo, staff members organize private transfers, get travelers and luggage to their private licensed car service in record time, and offer assistance through immigration and customs. The cost is $200 for the first person in a group and $75 for each additional person. During high season, this service should be booked as far in advance as possible, as there is limited availability.

Contacts **InterCaribbean Airways** ☎ 649/946–4181 ⊕ www. intercaribbean.com. **Caicos Express Airways** ☎ 649/941–5730, 305/677–3116 ⊕ caicosexpressairways.com. **VIP Flyers Club** ☎ 646/340–9602 in U.S., 649/946–4000 in Providenciales, 866/587–6168 toll-free ⊕ www.vipflyersclub.com.

AIRPORT TRANSFERS

Taxis are available after all arriving international flights. Few resorts are permitted to provide their own shuttle service, but most visitors are met at the airport by a repre-

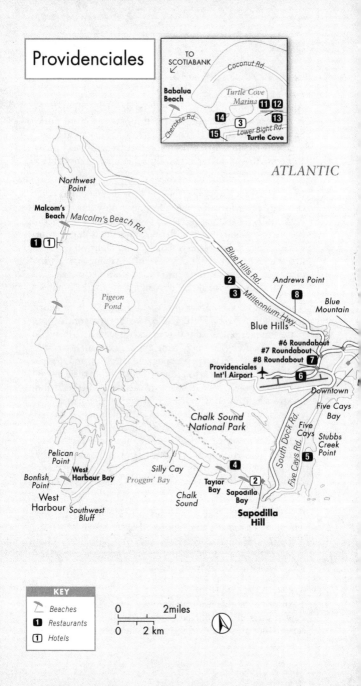

Providenciales

TO SCOTIABANK

Coconut Rd.

Babalua Beach

Turtle Cove Marina

Cherokee Rd.

14   **3**   **11** **12**
        13
15   Lower Bight Rd.
        Turtle Cove

ATLANTIC

Northwest Point

Malcom's Beach

Malcolm's Beach Rd.

1 **1**

Pigeon Pond

Blue Hills Rd.

2
3   Millennium Hwy.

Andrews Point   **8**

Blue Mountain

Blue Hills

#6 Roundabout
#7 Roundabout
#8 Roundabout   **7**

Providenciales Int'l Airport   **6**

Downtown

Five Cays Bay

Chalk Sound National Park

South Dock Rd.

Five Cays

Stubbs Creek Point

Pelican Point

West Harbour Bay

Silly Cay

Proggin' Bay

4

Bonfish Point

West Harbour   *Southwest Bluff*

Chalk Sound

Taylor Bay   **2**
        Sapodilla Bay

Five Cays Rd.

5

Sapodilla Hill

KEY

- Beaches
- **1** Restaurants
- **1** Hotels

0   2miles
0   2 km

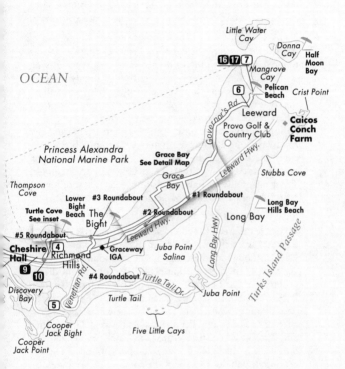

Water Cay

Little Water Cay

Donna Cay

Half Moon Bay

16 17 7

Mangrove Cay

6

Pelican Beach

Crist Point

OCEAN

Leeward

Caicos Conch Farm

Provo Golf & Country Club

Princess Alexandra National Marine Park

Grace Bay
See Detail Map

Grace Bay

#1 Roundabout

Stubbs Cove

Thompson Cove

Lower Bight Beach

#3 Roundabout

The Bight

#2 Roundabout

Long Bay Hills Beach

Turtle Cove
See inset

Long Bay

#5 Roundabout

Leeward Hwy.

Juba Point Salina

Cheshire Hall

4

Richmond Hills

Graceway IGA

Turks Island Passage

9

10

#4 Roundabout

Turtle Tail Dr.

Juba Point

Discovery Bay

5

Venetian Rd.

Turtle Tail

Cooper Jack Bight

Five Little Cays

Cooper Jack Point

Hotels

Amanyara, **1**

The Atrium, **6**

Blue Haven Resort and Marina, **7**

Harbour Club Villas, **5**

La Vista Azul, **4**

Neptune Villas, **2**

Turtle Cove Inn, **3**

Restaurants

Angela's Top o' the Cove, **10**

Baci Ristorante, **11**

Bugaloo's, **5**

Caribbean Cuisine, **6**

Da Conch Shack, **8**

Fire & Ice, **16**

Greenbean, **13**

Homey's, **7**

Kalooki's, **3**

Las Brisas, **4**

Magnolia Wine Bar & Restaurant, **15**

Mis Amigos, **9**

The Restaurantat Amanyara, **1**

Salt, **17**

Sharkbites Bar & Grill, **12**

Three Queens, **2**

Tiki Hut, **14**

sentative of their resort or villa and then connected with a regular taxi service. Many guests choose to rent a car; rental companies will have your rental waiting for you at the airport. Cabs are expensive, making car rentals an attractive alternative for those expecting to visit a variety of restaurants during their stay or do any exploration around the island.

A word of caution: the roads on Provo can be dangerous to navigate. Many tourists do not have experience driving on the left. Drinking and driving, though highly discouraged, does happen—some people forget they must follow the rules when they are relaxed and on vacation. Therefore, when driving on Provo—especially during busy season—be sure to take care. Look both ways before entering any roadway. Take a deep breath and enter roundabouts very carefully. Wear seat belts at all times, and be sure to ask your rental agency if there is coverage on your vehicle. There is not always liability insurance, as is mandatory in North America, and it's not included with your credit card.

BOAT AND FERRY TRAVEL

Ferries leave from Provo to North Caicos several times a day, and from there you can rent a car to explore Middle Caicos, though all these arrangements should be made in advance—especially during peak season to avoid disappointment. Caribbean Cruisin' also runs a ferry between Provo and South Caicos twice a week; the trip can be daunting for those a little queasy on the water, because the current can be rough. Ferry transfers between Grand Turk and Salt Cay can be iffy because of weather and water conditions, but there are other shared opportunities if you ask around. If you do wish to try the community ferry service, know that you may have to contact one of the restaurants or a dive operation to track the operator down.

Contacts **Caribbean Cruisin'** ✉ *Walkin Marina, Leeward, Providenciales* ☎ *649/946–5406, 649/231–4191* ⊕ *www.tciferry.com.* **Salt Cay Ferry** ✉ *Salt Cay* ☎ *649/231–6663* ⊕ *www.turksandcaicoswhalewatching.com.*

CAR TRAVEL

It is possible to stay on Providenciales for a week without renting a car if you are willing to rely on very expensive taxis, a bicycle, or your own two feet to get around. There are certainly many wonderful restaurants and shops within walking distance in the Grace Bay area, but for those staying away from the main hub, that is just not the case. Also, tour operators will do pickups only in the Grace Bay area. Therefore, it's advisable to plan to rent a car for at least a few days so that you'll have the flexibility to explore independently and be able to access restaurants and services that may be farther afield. Driving is on the left—British-style!

Signage for roads on Provo can be hard to come by, but locals use the island's roundabouts as their landmarks. Once you get a feel for those, driving around the island becomes less daunting than it might be at first. The following list gives you an idea of what you are looking for when trying to navigate the island. *See the Providenciales map for more information on where these are.*

Here is a complete list:

1. Rubis (This is at the far end of the divided highway with Seven Stars on the oceanfront.)

2. Thomas Stubbs Roundabout (More aptly described as the Beaches Resort turnoff, this one has a sign for the resort front and center in the manicured circle.)

3. Graceway IGA Supermarket

4. Felix Morley Roundabout (Leading down Venetian Road to Turtle Tail is another Rubis not far from the main IGA, with nothing in its center and looking a bit war torn.)

5. Suzy Turn (Don't run through this tiny roundabout across from Napa Auto Parts; this one has a stop sign!)

6. Five Cays and Chalk Sound Roundabout (There's no sign for this one, but it's heading down the hill. You will see a giant red gift at Christmastime to mark the spot; it is one of the more traditional wide circles.)

7. Fuller Walkin Roundabout (This one is for Blue Hills. It is a bit tricky to navigate and is found at the entrance to downtown.)

8. Walter Cox Roundabout (It's an alternative to Five Cays, South Dock Road, and Chalk Sound in one direction; head in the opposite one for the airport. It is landscaped and has a TCI artistic representation on the wall in the center.)

EXPLORING PROVIDENCIALES

Although you may be quite content to enjoy the beaches and top-notch amenities of Provo's resorts, there are certainly plenty of activities beyond the resorts. Provo is a great starting point for island-hopping tours by sea or by air as well as fishing and diving trips. Resurfaced roads make for easy travel.

GRACE BAY

The "hub" of the island is the stunning Grace Bay Beach, a graceful curve of soft sand along Provo's north shore. Between it and the Lower Bight Road, which runs parallel to the beach, are many shops, restaurants, and resorts, the majority of what is to be found on the island. There are sidewalks and streetlights, cafés and coffee shops, restaurants, spas, tour operators, and a variety of specialty stores. This area is where the majority of tourists stay, especially for their first visit to the island.

THE BIGHT

This beach area is popular for off-the-beach snorkeling and an even more popular Thursday night fish fry. The Provo Sailing Club meets most Saturdays at The Bight Park for sailing lessons or family picnics. There is no defining where The Bight starts and Grace Bay ends, so most just assume that it is simply the "quiet end" of Grace Bay.

TURTLE COVE

The Bight Beach eventually blends into the beach around the opening to Turtle Cove. Inland, around the marina that harbors many of the fishing charters and smaller private yachts, is where you will find several excursion companies and fishing charters, as well as a couple of popular restaurants, including Sharkbite and Baci Restaurante.

LEEWARD

An upscale residential area, Leeward is the eastward extension of the island. Yes, it is possible to stroll right off the end of Grace Bay proper and onto the more quiet stretch of Pelican Beach, where you'll find a few quite grand residences and villa rentals. Working your way around the point, you can look across Leeward Channel to Little Water

TOP REASONS TO GO

Grace Bay Beach. This beach is the Turks and Caicos' biggest draw. The soft, powder-white sand with crystal-clear seas seems to go on for as far as the eye can see. Although it is often touted as a 12-mile (19-km) stretch, one can stroll just over 3 miles (5 km) in one direction before coming across the entry to Turtle Cove and Thompson Cove—in which you would have to swim to get around it. Not to worry, those 3 miles can take a person all day, as you will want to stop, take a dip, enjoy a drink, or have a bite to eat.

Snorkel, Scuba, and Snuba. The world's third-largest reef system here makes for an underwater dream. Beginners and experts alike can snorkel right off the shoreline on the Bight Reef, Smith's Reef, and off Babalua Beach. The visibility is ideal, usually more than 100 feet. If you aren't a certified diver, Snuba is a choice for you; the tanks stay on the surface while you explore below.

Fine Dining. On quiet islands like Provo dining is your nightlife. And although the food is incredible across the island, what really stands out is the variety of settings. Infiniti of Grace Bay Club, formerly known as Anacaona, ranks at the top with one of the most beautiful settings in the Caribbean. If you are lucky enough, nothing is finer than the chic minimalist bar and restaurant at Amanyara.

Water Sports. For most people, Turks and Caicos is all about the water, and not always what's below the surface. On Grace Bay you can parasail, ride a banana boat, sail a Hobie Cat, take out a kayak or paddleboard, or learn to windsurf. Long Bay Beach is the newest hot spot for kite surfers; you will find dozens out enjoying the wind every day of the week. The more protected waters off Leeward and the cays are great for waterskiing, wakeboarding, and tubing. Big Blue Unlimited also has kayak and paddleboard rentals there, so you can explore the mangroves and beyond.

The Perfect Night Out. At sunset, have a drink anywhere along Grace Bay Beach, whether at one of the many seaside bars or restaurants or with a bottle you have uncorked in your very own private condo. Stay and enjoy dinner there, or move along to another. Be sure to enjoy some live music along the way; local musicians can be found at various spots throughout the week. Late on Friday night you can enjoy a bit of dancing at the Ganzevoort, Grace Bay's only nightlife,.

2

CLOSE UP Providenciales in One Day

If you are en route to one of the family islands, or have booked a stay along Grace Bay and not imagined to venture off the resort, perhaps you should consider renting a car to explore Provo for just a day. Starting at the far eastern end of the island, you can visit Provo's Conch Farm, the only one in the world. While you're there, you'll be able to say hello to a couple of resident conchs. If you are not staying on the island, be sure to take a quick detour through Grace Bay, checking out the beach for future visits and perhaps a couple of the shops. Coming down the island, history buffs might stop at Cheshire Hall. Here are the remnants of an old plantation within walking distance off Leeward Highway. From there, carry on to Chalk Sound; it is definitely an island must-see. The water here is shallow and bright with small islands dotted throughout the middle; the sight truly takes your breath away. While you are out there, be sure to stop at Las Brisas at Neptune Villas. The location offers stunning views of the sound, and it's a perfect spot for lunch and a refreshment. If you are willing and able, you can take one of their rental kayaks for an hour—or longer. But if you are looking for a beach by this time, then Sapodilla and Taylor bays are just a little way beyond; the waters are shallow for hundreds of feet, making them a child's dream. Backtrack to downtown and take a ride to Malcolm's Beach out at Northwest Point, and then finish your day off in Blue Hills, where colorful buildings are the setting for a game of "slamming" dominos and a few local restaurants serve up wonderful Caribbean cuisine, all on the beach with unobstructed views of the sun as it sets.

Cay, home of the rock iguana. Stop there, as the shoreline gets rocky and the mangroves soon begin. It is not possible to continue along unless you cut through private property. At the easternmost end of the island are the Heaving Down Rock and Walkin marinas, accessible only by boat and by car. This is where the ferry to North and South Caicos is based.

FAMILY **Caicos Conch Farm.** More than 3 million conchs are farmed at this commercial operation on the northeast tip of Provo, as well as the breeding stock for four different freshwater fish for future farming. It's a popular tourist attraction, too, with guided tours and a small gift shop selling conch-related souvenirs, jewelry, and freshwater pearls. You can even meet Jerry and Sally, the resident conchs that are brought out on demand. ⊠ *Leeward-Going-Through, Leeward* ☎ *649/946–5330* ⊕ *www.caicosconchfarm.net/* ☜ *$12* ⊙ *Weekdays 9–4, Sat. 9–2:30.*

VENETIAN ROAD

Behind the Graceway IGA supermarket on Leeward Highway, this major road leads to the beaches and villas of Turtle Tail. At times it's a great spot to observe several visiting flamingos as they feed in Turtle and Flamingo lakes. This is a lovely road to take an early-morning run, as it is flat and parallels the water, with little traffic. From Leeward Highway to the end is approximately 6 miles (10 km).

TURTLE TAIL

Look south, out to the ocean behind Graceway IGA, and you'll see homes dotted along a ridgeline. Turtle Tail is the long spit of land that curves around on the south side of the island, and the beauty of the Caicos Banks lies in front of the homes. Although centrally located, it is one of the quietest areas of the island, and the location of many stunning vacation villas.

DISCOVERY BAY

The point of land across the bay from Turtle Tail and the south-side marinas is called Discovery Bay, where there is another ridge with several vacation homes. If you drive out to the end, you can hike out and put your nose in the wind. Five small cays just offshore are the perfect contrast to the mesmerizing blues of the Caicos Banks, making this picture perfect.

DOWNTOWN

Although there are some businesses concentrated here, downtown is primarily a commercial area near the airport that does not offer much for tourists. Close by, however, are the ruins of an old plantation.

Cheshire Hall. Standing eerily just east of downtown Provo are the remains of an 18th-century cotton plantation owned by the loyalist Thomas Stubbs. A trail weaves through the ruins, where a few interpretive signs tell the story of the island's doomed cotton industry, with little information about the plantation itself. A variety of local plants are also

Taxi Fares on Providenciales

Taxi fares are expensive on Provo. Rates are published in a schedule, which is based on distance. Knowing approximate fares in advance may help you decide if you want to rent a car or enjoy the freedom of not having to think. Just remember that all taxi fares are based on two people traveling and include two pieces of luggage each. Extra luggage is an additional charge (golf bags are $5 each), but grocery bags are free. Kids under 12 traveling with an adult are half rate, and if a taxi is left standing at the grocery store or elsewhere, the first 10 minutes may be complimentary—depending on the driver—and after that there will be a 60¢ per minute wait charge. Here are some approximate fares based on two people traveling together from the airport; the fee for each additional person is half the published fare:

Turtle Cove: $16

Discovery Bay (Graceway IGA or South Dock): $20

The Bight (Coral Gardens or Reef Residences): $23

The Bight (Beaches): $27

West Grace Bay (Sibonné, Alexandra, Sands, Somerset, Point Grace, Villa Renaissance, Regent Grand, or Saltmills): $28

Mid-Grace Bay (Grace Bay Club, Seven Stars, Graceway Gourmet, Coco Bistro): $33

Grace Bay (Ocean Club West, Caribbean Paradise Inn, Ports of Call): $33

Long Bay: $36

Upper Chalk Sound: $36

East Grace Bay (Ocean Club, Tuscany, Royal West Indies, Club Med): $40

Leeward (Conch Farm, Marina): $43

Lower Chalk Sound, Silly Creek: $48

Northwest Point (for Amanyara): $86

---

identified. A short tour by an associate from the Turks & Caicos National Trust will fill in the historical details for history buffs. Contact the Trust to visit; there's a nominal fee that goes toward preserving the nation's heritage. If this piques your interest, a visit to the North Caicos Wades Green plantation or the Turks and Caicos National Museum in Grand Turk will provide more of the story. ⊠ *Leeward Hwy., across from Royal Jewels, Downtown* ☎ *649/941–5710 for National Trust* ☜ *$10* ☉ *Weekdays 8:30–4:30, Sat. 9–1 (guided tour required).*

AIRPORT

Aside from the airport itself, there's not much to attract tourists. Along the road between downtown and the airport proper you'll find some great little local restaurants, however, and some interesting beauty supply shops and department-like stores. If you are stuck without a suitcase for a few days, this might be the area where you'll find many of your basics at a much reduced cost.

FIVE CAYS

The biggest attraction in this relatively less fortunate community is the ever-popular Bugaloo's. Go on a Sunday afternoon for some lively fun when the whole island seems to turn up, or enjoy it seven days a week as a spot with lots of local flavor. Five Cays is also home to Provo's fishery. Keep to the left after passing Bugaloo's, and you'll find the spot to purchase fresh conch and lobster—when in season. These are cash transactions only, and note that it is open only for the two hours before sunset when the boats come in, on days when the ocean is calm enough for the boats to go out.

CHALK SOUND

You will first see the beauty of Chalk Sound on approach into Providenciales' airport. At the end of the runway, this protected body of water dotted with wee islands creates your first impression of the Turks and Caicos Islands. You will never lay eyes on anything lovelier.

Chalk Sound National Park. As you drive out to the end of South Dock Road, on your right you'll catch glimpses of Chalk Sound. The water here seems luminescent. There are a couple of places to stop for pictures, but carry on until you can turn off on Chalk Sound Drive. You can enjoy lunch overlooking the park at Las Brisas Restaurant or drive to the very end of the road and take a walk along the shoreline where there are no homes—yet. No matter how many times you see it, it still manages to take your breath away. ⊠ *Chalk Sound Rd., Chalk Sound.*

FAMILY **Sapodilla Hill.** On this hilltop overlooking the beauty of Sapodilla Bay you might find what is left of several rock carvings. It is thought that sailors carved the names and dates into the rocks while they watched over their ships

On a Budget in the TCI

CLOSE UP

If you would like to visit one of the world's most beautiful beaches but feel you can't afford this expensive destination, there are ways to save money in the Turks and Caicos and still have a wonderful trip. Traveling during nonpeak season, when many resorts offer free nights and extra perks, is one way to save. The discount season coincides with hurricane season, June through November, so consider purchasing travel insurance if you visit then. If you don't mind being a block or two from the beach, you can even save more. And staying in one of the many private villas does not always mean higher prices. In fact, there are lovely little homes dotted all over the island that are more than comfortable, with only a short drive to all that Provo has to offer. You might also look at searching for package deals that combine air, accommodation, and even diving.

Most resort rooms and condos, as well as all private villas, have at least a refrigerator and microwave, so you can stock up at the supermarket and prepare some of your meals "at home." Graceway IGA has an awesome rotisserie chicken and prepared pasta and potato salads. Visit the Graceway Gourmet for an amazing deli that almost doesn't make it worth it to purchase anything that needs preparing. Also, airlines allow you to bring a cooler of food as long as perishables are frozen and vacuum sealed; despite airline charges for checked bags, this strategy could save you some money, especially on meat.

At restaurants, dinner might be more expensive than for the same entrée at lunchtime, so arrive 15 minutes before the switch-over and order from the lunch menu. You can pick up pizza or another island takeout meal and have a balcony picnic. There are also several little local haunts throughout Grace Bay, as well as along Airport Road that are not nearly as expensive. To be sure, ordering nonalcoholic beverages while out will save a great deal of money.

And of course, many of the best experiences are free: walk the beach, swim in the ocean, snorkel where the reef comes in to touch the shore. The options are endless. A good source for events and specials is ⊕ *www. TCIEnews.com.*

from a high vantage point, perhaps while the hulls were being cleaned or repairs were being made. The details are uncertain, but they have been dated back to the mid-1700s to mid-1800s. You will see replicas displayed at Provo's

International Airport. ⊠ *Off South Dock Rd., west of South Dock, Chalk Sound.*

WEST HARBOUR

Otherwise known as Pirates' Cove, West Harbour offers small caves, Osprey Rock, and rock carvings that all make this an enticing place to explore. On a secluded southwest part of the island, it's a long drive out, and the parking lot has had some break-ins, so be sure to stow your belongings out of sight and lock your car.

BLUE MOUNTAIN

Many gorgeous private villas with ocean views can be found here. The beaches are smaller and more private than those elsewhere on the island, and although it's in a central location, visitors staying here will require transportation to reach the best beaches.

BLUE HILLS

The "personality" of the island, this area populated with locals is west, beyond Grace Bay and Turtle Cove. The beachfront is lined with quirky beach shacks and colorful restaurants. It's a place to "chill" with water views, but no one ever swims here, because there are better areas for hanging out on the sand. The beachcombing is much better than on Grace Bay, however, as there surely isn't anyone raking the sand! This is where you will find Da Conch Shack and Kalooki's.

NORTHWEST POINT

The farthest point northwest on the island, this is a great scuba spot with one secluded resort. The Northwest Point Resort is a long way from everything, but the beaches are amazing—albeit wild—and the Northwest Point Nature Reserve is tucked in behind.

BEACHES

Everyone comes for Grace Bay, with its miles of clean, powdery sand and the contrasting hues of unimaginably turquoise water set against the deep blues over the reef, but you should not overlook Provo's other beaches, each with its own unique allure. Although some beaches require effort to reach, they will definitely be worth the trek. On the rare chance that chop arises on Grace Bay, you can always head to the other side of Provo for calm and shallower waters. An additional bonus? There are no vendors on any of the beaches to interrupt your relaxation.

GRACE BAY

★ Fodor'sChoice **Grace Bay.** The world-famous sweeping stretch of ivory-white, powder-soft sand on Provo's north shore is simply breathtaking. It's home to migrating starfish as well as shallow snorkeling trails. The majority of Provo's beachfront resorts are along this shore, and it's the primary reason why the Turks and Caicos are a world-class destination. **Amenities:** food and drink; parking (free); water sports. **Best for:** sunset; swimming; walking. ⊠ *Grace Bay Rd., along the north shore, Grace Bay.*

THE BIGHT

Lower Bight Beach. Lower Bight Beach is often confused with Grace Bay Beach because it seems to blend right into it. The beach is gorgeous and has a slightly wilder, more natural setting. It also has off-the-beach snorkeling. The Provo Sailing Club gives lessons most Saturdays for the residents of the island but also holds the Annual Fools Regatta in June, which everyone can enjoy. There's also a kids' park right nearby. **Amenities:** food and drink; parking (free). **Best for:** snorkeling; walking. ⊠ *Lower Bight Rd., Grace Bay.*

LEEWARD

Pelican Beach. This beautiful stretch of beach blends right into Grace Bay Beach, with little distinction between where one ends and the other begins. Because of a cut in the reef, Pelican Beach has wonderful shells to enjoy—but remember that you are in part of a national park, so they must be left behind for others to see long after you have gone home. Chances are you'll be the only one on this beautiful strand. Enjoy. **Amenities:** parking (free). **Best for:** solitude; walking. ⊠ *Sandpiper Ave., Leeward ✦ At Grace Bay Road and Seven Stars, keep straight on Grace Bay Road until you pass an unmanned gatehouse. At the big circle take your first left, Sandpiper Avenue. At the small roundabout take a left until the road ends, and park. The beach blends with Leeward Beach and Grace Bay on the left; on the right, walk around to Pelican Beach.*

BIG WATER CAY

★ Fodors Choice **Half Moon Bay.** This natural ribbon of sand links two uninhabited cays; it's only inches above the sparkling turquoise waters and one of the most gorgeous beaches on the island. There are limestone cliffs to explore as well as small, sandy coves; there's even a small wreck offshore for snorkeling. It's only a short boat ride away from Provo, and most of the island's tour companies run excursions here or simply offer a beach drop-off. These companies include Silverdeep and Caicos Dream Tours *(⇨ Boating and Sailing, in Sports and the Outdoors)*. **Amenities:** none. **Best for:** solitude; snorkeling; swimming; walking. ⊠ *Between Big Water Cay and Little Water Cay, Little Water Cay.*

LONG BAY

Long Bay Hills Beach. On the southeastern end of the island, visitors will find this a lovely stretch to stroll. It's not much of a place to swim, as the water is shallow and shells litter the floor. This is where you can pick up a conch shell to take home, as it is not part of the country's park system. It's ungroomed, so you'll find many along the shore. Long Bay is also where some will have their dreams of riding horseback fulfilled. The guides with Provo Ponies will also let them swim. Of course, the kitesurfers have also made this their mecca. On any given Saturday- there may be up to a hundred kiters enjoying the shallower waters and warm trade winds to advance their skills and ride their cares away. If you're not a participant, come out and enjoy the show. You can watch world-class boarders daily. It might spark some interest so that you find yourself checking in with one of the several instructors giving lessons out on Long Bay. **Amenities:** parking (free). **Best for:** walking; windsurfing; kitesurfing. ⊠ *Long Bay Rd., Long Bay ⊹ On Leeward Highway, continue onto its "extension" as if traveling to Walkin Marina. Watch on the right for the entrance to the Shore Club. Follow this road until you get to the public access point next to their parking lot.*

CHALK SOUND

Sapodilla Bay. One of the best of the many secluded beaches around Provo is this peaceful quarter-mile cove protected by Sapodilla Hill. The soft strand here is lapped by calm waves, and yachts and small boats move with the gentle tide. During low tide little sandbar "islands" form—they're great for a beach chair. **Amenities:** parking (free). **Best for:** walking. ⊠ *End of South Dock Rd., Chalk Sound* ✛ *From Leeward Highway, take Roundabout 6 at the bottom of the Leeward Highway hill toward Five Cays. Follow until almost the end, and at the small police station turn right onto Chalk Sound Road. The first dirt road on the left leads to a small parking area.*

Taylor Bay. Taylor Bay is shallow for hundreds of feet, making it a perfect place for kids; they become giddy at the fact that they can run free through shallow waters without their parents worrying about them. The beach also offers gorgeous views of the villas that hang over the shoreline on one side of the bay here. As it has had many amazing reviews over the years, don't expect to have this one all to yourself. There is even the odd tour that pulls up. **Amenities:** none. **Best for:** solitude; wading. ⊠ *Sunset Dr., Chalk Sound* ✛ *From Leeward Highway take Roundabout 6 toward Five Cays. Follow the road until almost the end, and at the small police station, take a right onto Chalk Sound Road. Take a left at Ocean Point Drive and park next to the tennis courts where there are big boulders blocking a sand path. Follow this path to the beach.*

GLOWWORMS. **If you're here on the third to fifth days after a full moon, you might get to see glowworms. The phenomenon occurs when tiny marine worms mate. You have to time it perfectly to see their dance, as the show lasts only a half hour at most. Magically, the female begins to glow, waiting patiently for a male to notice. If one does, his colors are shown as he dashes in for the "explosion," resulting in what appears like stars twinkling at dusk across the water's surface. The best places to view them from land are along the canals that open onto the Caicos Banks and within the Chalk Sound residential neighborhoods. You can also choose to view them from an excursion boat.**

NORTHWEST POINT

Malcolm's Beach. It's one of the most stunning beaches you'll ever see, but you'll need to drive carefully, as the road is a little rough in spots. Bring your own food and drinks, because there are no facilities for miles around. There have been reports of break-ins at the parking lot in years past, so it's best not to keep any valuables in your car or on your person, and never go alone. **Amenities:** parking (free). **Best**

for: solitude; swimming; walking. ⊠ *Malcolm's Beach Rd.,*
beyond the Amanyara turnoff, Northwest Point ⊹ *On Lee-*
ward Highway, take the Fuller Walkin roundabout toward
Blue Hills. Keep to the main highway until after it turns
into rolled packed sand. Take the second unpaved road on
the left. Follow the road until the end, which takes about
20 minutes. There is a rough patch that requires caution.

WEST HARBOUR

West Harbour Bay. This is about as isolated as it gets on
Provo. West Bay has long stretches of beaches to walk and
explore, and there's no other person in sight for hours.
Occasionally Captain Bill's Outback Adventure excursion
stops here and explores the nearby pirate caves. Not only
can you occasionally find large red starfish in the water
here, but taking a walk out to Bonefish Point might mean
you will spot small reef sharks and the odd ray hunting in
the shallows. **Amenities:** none. **Best for:** solitude; walking.
⊠ *West Harbour.*

WHERE TO EAT

Dining options on Provo are numerous. Without a doubt,
there must be close to a hundred restaurants on the island,
each with its individual ambience and style of food. As the
Caribbean has attracted travelers from around the globe
since the time of Christopher Columbus, these influences
come through in the foods of the region. Today you will
experience a hint of Moroccan, Thai, Spanish, and Indian
flavors, to name but a few.

There's everything from small beach shacks with the freshest seafood right off the boats to elegant restaurants with
extensive wine lists. Most of the restaurants that cater to
tourists offer numerous choices, with a little bit of everything on the menu. Don't like seafood? Have chicken or
beef. Don't like spice? Ask for the tamer version. Vegetarian? Need kid-friendly food? Feel free to ask for something
that's not on the menu; most of the island's chefs will try
to accommodate requests. Some restaurants will also set
up a table on the beach surrounded by tiki torches for that
special occasion. Restaurants on Provo are generally upscale
and expensive; you will find no fast-food chains here. As
an option, there are excellent caterers on the island, too.
The sky's the limit. Invite one such as Kissing Fish Catering to pack you a picnic lunch, prepare a pig roast on the

beach, or come in to prepare an exquisite dinner in your private villa.

The best local food on the island is conch, which you will find everywhere prepared in many different ways. You may find it as ceviche, as ceviche in a salad, as deep-fried conch fingers, in spicy conch fritters, or as the base in a hearty conch chowder. It is also often found as part of fresh seafood specials, with colorful presentation and a tangy dose of spice.

Some restaurants do close during the slow season, with dates fluctuating yearly—usually from late August through late October. On the rare rainy day—or an unusually hot day—there are even a few indoor restaurants, complete with air-conditioning, as noted in the individual reviews.

Pick up a free copy of *WhereWhenHow's Dining Guide*, which you can find all over the island—or check out their website; it contains menus, website addresses, and pictures of all the restaurants.

WHAT IT COSTS IN U.S. DOLLARS			
$	**$$**	**$$$**	**$$$$**
Restaurants under $12	$12–$20	$21–$30	over $30

Prices in the restaurant reviews are the average cost of a main course at dinner or, if dinner is not served, at lunch; taxes and service charges are generally included.

GRACE BAY

★ Fodor's Choice ✕ **Bay Bistro.** *International.* You simply can't eat
$$$$ any closer to the beach than here at Bay Bistro, directly
FAMILY on Grace Bay Beach. You have the option of dining on a covered deck, on an open-air patio, or with your feet in the sand, surrounded by palm trees with the sound of lapping waves. The coffee-rubbed tuna appetizer—with a hint of wasabi—is the best. Their fish-and-chips are quite lovely, and for the carnivore, the beef tenderloin is to die for. Seasonally, lobster is brought to their back door daily by local fishermen. End the evening with homemade ice cream. Their weekend brunches include such favorites as eggs Benedict—one of the few places on island to find it—with mimosas included. Be sure to reserve if you are coming with a large group, as it is quite a popular way to begin a lazy day. Around the time of the full moon, ask about the memorable beach barbecue: grilled shrimp, roast suckling

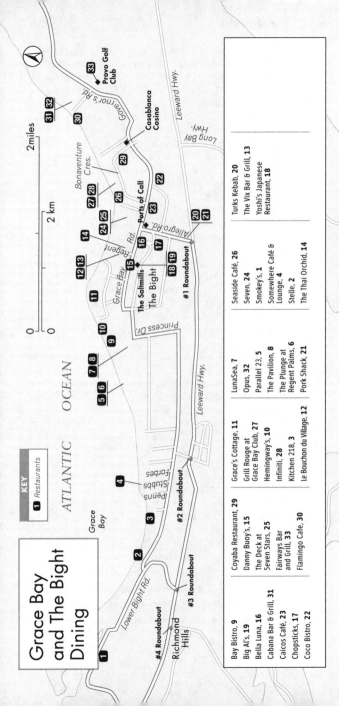

Grace Bay and The Bight Dining

ATLANTIC OCEAN

Grace Bay

KEY

⬛ Restaurants

Penns Stubbs Forbes

Princess Dr.

Leeward Hwy.

Lower Bight Rd.

Richmond Hills

#4 Roundabout

#3 Roundabout

#2 Roundabout

#1 Roundabout

Grace Bay Rd.

Regent Rd.

The Salmills

The Bight

Ports of Call

Allegro Rd.

Bonaventure Cres.

Governor's Rd.

Leeward Hwy.

Long Bay Hwy.

Casablanca Casino

Provo Golf Club

2 miles

2 km

Bay Bistro, **9**
Big Al's, **19**
Bella Luna, **16**
Cabana Bar & Grill, **31**
Caicos Café, **23**
Chopsticks, **17**
Coco Bistro, **22**

Coyaba Restaurant, **29**
Danny Buoy's, **15**
The Deck at Seven Stars, **25**
Fairways Bar and Grill, **33**
Flamingo Cafe, **30**

Grace's Cottage, **11**
Grill Rouge at Grace Bay Club, **27**
Hemingway's, **10**
Infiniti, **28**
Kitchen 218, **3**
Le Bouchon du Village, **12**

LunaSea, **7**
Opus, **32**
Parallel 23, **5**
The Pavilion, **8**
The Plunge at Regent Palms, **6**
Pork Shack, **21**

Seaside Café, **26**
Seven, **24**
Smokey's, **1**
Somewhere Café & Lounge, **4**
Stelle, **2**
The Thai Orchid, **14**

Turks Kebab, **20**
The Vix Bar & Grill, **13**
Yoshi's Japanese Restaurant, **18**

pig, side fixings—all enjoyed while sitting around a wonderful bonfire on the beach. ⑤ *Average main: $35* ⊠ *Sibonné Beach Hotel, Princess Dr., Grace Bay* ☎ *649/946–5396* ⊕ *sibonne.com/grace-bay-bistro* ⌕ *Reservations essential.*

$$$ ╳ **Bella Luna Ristorante.** *Italian.* For wonderfully traditional Italian food, this restaurant, which is a converted private house set one block back from the beach, is elevated so that diners may enjoy ocean breezes and views of Grace Bay. Ground level is their intimate pizza place, offering one of the only authentic wood-oven pizzas on island. (Your children will love the Nutella calzones for dessert.) You sit in the gardens, which are threaded with fairy lights at night. Veal, fish, and chicken dishes are made with fresh herbs and wine-cream sauces, olive oil, and lemon butter. One of the best dishes on the menu is the Vitello Boscaiola, topped with portobello mushrooms in a Marsala sauce and served with a side of homemade pasta. It's absolutely delicious. If lobster Fra Diavolo is not on the menu, ask for it. But be warned: it's hot. There's also a three-course prix-fixe menu for less than $35, consisting of the appetizer, a main dish, and a bite-size dessert. ⑤ *Average main: $30* ⊠ *The Glass House, Grace Bay Rd., Grace Bay* ☎ *649/946–5214* ⊘ *Closed Sun. No lunch.*

$$ ╳ **Big Al's Island Grill.** *Burger.* This laid-back diner is at Salt Mills Plaza. You'll find a huge selection of burgers here, including the Pretzel Burger, served in a pretzel bun, or the Hawaiian Volcano Island Burger with grilled pineapple, jalapeno, teriyaki glaze, and Jack cheese. If you dare, there's Big Al's Tomahawk Burger, topped with smoked bacon, grilled onions, melted cheddar, cholula sauce, and fried egg. Hungry diners can try the Big Al's Slider Challenge. If you can down 12 sliders, 18 onion rings, and a drink all in 30 minutes, you get yourself on their Wall of Fame and go home with a Slider Challenge T-shirt. Of course there are other options for non–burger lovers. There are also wraps, pastas, salads, and vegan and vegetarian options. It's a great spot for family dining. ⑤ *Average main: $15* ⊠ *Salt Mills Plaza, Grace Bay* ☎ *649/941–3797* ⊕ *www.big alsislandgrill.com* ⌕ *Reservations not accepted.*

ROMANCE ON THE BEACH. **Is there a more romantic way to celebrate a special occasion than with a wonderful dinner by the water with your feet in the sand? There are a couple of options where you may dine at a table set on the shoreline, complete with tiki**

CLOSE UP

Provo's Thursday Fish Fry

On Thursday night you can enjoy local cuisine from multiple restaurants in one place. Residents and tourists alike gather for the lively atmosphere, great ambience, and chance to see the island's culture expressed in the Junkanoo—a local dancing band extravaganza. The smells from the grills will keep you hungry, so it's a great way to compare who makes the best local dishes. Hole in the Wall and Smokey's are just two of the weekly participants. It's fun for the whole family, and the convenient location means that you don't have to leave the main tourist area to try some of the best local cuisine.

torches, candles, and tablecloths. **Bay Bistro** and **Kissing Fish Catering** are two of the places to turn to for that special evening.

$$ ✕**Cabana Bar & Grille.** *American.* This is a great option if you're looking for a quick lunch with a view of beautiful Grace Bay Beach just steps away. The food is simple and good, featuring such basic fare as hamburgers and wraps. Of course you'll find conch dishes and other local specialties as well. The restaurant features nightly specials: Wednesday night is Rib Night, Friday night is Jerk Night, and Sunday is Kabob Day. There are nightly happy hours, and live music takes center stage on certain evenings— check with the restaurant to find out who is featured and when. ⑤ *Average main: $15* ✉ *Ocean Club, Grace Bay Rd., Grace Bay* ☎ *649/946–5880* ⊕ *www.oceanclubresorts.com* ⚠ *Reservations not accepted.*

$$$$ ✕**Caicos Café Bar and Grill.** *Italian.* Here the island dishes come with an Italian twist. Everything is fresh and carefully prepared. The bread is even baked fresh daily at the bakery next door. A favorite of residents is the Mediterranean-style seafood casserole, made with white wine and a light tomato sauce. This restaurant is also a good option for vegetarians. On windy nights the inland setting offers protection from the breezes, and the large flamboyant tree is quite spectacular, especially when it is in full bloom. (Bug spray may be necessary at night.) ⑤ *Average main: $32* ✉ *Caicos Café Plaza, Grace Bay Rd., Grace Bay* ☎ *649/946–5278* ⚠ *caicoscafe@tciway.tc* ☉ *Closed Sun.*

$$ ✕ **Chopsticks.** *Asian.* It's been a while since there has been a Chinese restaurant on Provo, but Chopsticks is here to stay. You have the choice of sitting along the street in the more family-friendly, picnic-table-style seating, in the more ambient courtyard plaza surrounded by rockwork and fairy lights, or inside with AC. Try the crab-and-goat-cheese wontons as an appetizer, any of their three hakka noodles as your main, or the Sliced Fish in Oyster Chili Sauce as a seafood entrée. Of course there are a number of curries, and chicken and beef dishes. Ⓢ *Average main: $18* ✉ *Neptune Plaza, Grace Bay* ☎ *649/333–4040* ⊕ *www.facebook.com/ chopstickstci* ⊙ *never.*

★ Fodor'sChoice ✕ **Coco Bistro.** *International.* With tables exoti-
$$$$ cally set within a mature palm grove, Coco Bistro is one of the most popular restaurants on Provo. Main courses combine continental dishes with a Caribbean flair, and seafood abounds. Be sure to try their Caicos lobster bisque; it's flambé style with cognac and a hint of spicy cream. The roast rack of lamb with an herb crust is also amazing. This is a must-visit, so be sure to make reservations at least one week ahead during nonpeak season, two to three weeks ahead in peak season. Ⓢ *Average main: $40* ✉ *Grace Bay Rd., Grace Bay* ☎ *649/946–5369* ⊕ *www.CocoBistro.tc* ⚑ *Reservations essential* ⊙ *Closed Mon. No lunch.*

★ Fodor'sChoice ✕ **Coyaba Restaurant.** *International.* Directly
$$$$ behind Grace Bay Club at Caribbean Paradise Inn, this posh restaurant is in a palm-fringed setting. The nostalgic favorites here are served with tempting twists in conversation-piece crockery. Chef Paul Newman uses his culinary expertise for the daily-changing main courses, which include exquisitely presented dishes such as crispy, whole yellow snapper fried in Thai spices. One standout is lobster thermidor in a Dijon-mushroom cream sauce. You may want to try several different appetizers instead of an entrée for dinner; guava-and-tamarind barbecue ribs and coconut-shrimp tempura are two good choices if you go that route. If you enjoy creative menus, this is the place for you. Coyaba keeps the resident expat crowd happy with traditional favorites such as lemon meringue pie, albeit with his own tropical twist. Don't skip dessert; Paul makes incredible chocolate fondant. Ⓢ *Average main: $40* ✉ *Caribbean Paradise Inn, Bonaventure Crescent, off Grace Bay Rd., Grace Bay* ☎ *649/946–5186* ⊕ *www.coyabarestaurant. com* ⚑ *Reservations essential* ⊙ *Closed Tues. and Sept.–Oct.*

$$ ✕**Danny Buoy's.** *Irish.* A true local watering hole, this bar always has a mix of locals and vacationers. It was once your typical pub, where you could watch your favorite sport no matter what part of the world you were from. Now it not only attracts the armchair sports enthusiast, but is also jam-packed with slot machines. There are those who come here for the drinks—although they no longer have the range of beer on tap they once did—and entertainment factor, but also to dine on traditional Irish favorites such as fish-and-chips. This is one of the few places you'll always find open late. The inside is not recommended for families. If you have children along, go early and take a seat outdoors. ⑤ *Average main: $20* ⊠ *Grace Bay Rd., next to the Saltmills, Grace Bay* ☎ *649/946–5921* ⊕ *www.danny buoys.com* ⌕ *Reservations not accepted.*

$$$ ✕**The Deck at Seven Stars.** *Eclectic.* It's hard to think of a more alluring setting than The Deck, perched on the dunes overlooking the ocean at the Seven Stars resort. Tiki torches, fire pits, and awnings lend plenty of chic to this otherwise much more casual sister of the property's more formal restaurant, Seven. Nosh on small plates, or consider one of the fine lobster or pasta dishes. Be sure to save Sunday night for The Deck, as they host a sunset beach barbecue with live music. ⑤ *Average main: $22* ⊠ *Seven Stars Resort, Grace Bay Rd., Grace Bay* ☎ *649/339–3777* ⊕ *www.seven starsgracebay.com.*

★ Fodor'sChoice ✕**Fairways Bar & Grill.** *American.* Located at the
$$$$ Provo Golf and Country Club, Fairways is open seven days a week for breakfast and lunch, and on Friday night for dinner. Hot or cold breakfast is offered during the week, and the Sunday brunch features waffles and eggs Benedict. Lunches are snack-style bites along with an array of sandwiches and burgers. Currently, the talk is all about Asian Friday Night, when the Filipino chef creates a number of delicious dishes, including Thai red and green curries, as well as barbecue pork loin served on bamboo sticks. Golfers will enjoy the view down the fairways and over a green. On other nights there are rugby matches on the big screen. ⑤ *Average main: $35* ⊠ *Grace Bay Rd., Grace Bay* ☎ *649/946–5833* ✉ *fairways@provogolfclub.com* ⊕ *www. provogolfclub.com.*

$$ ✕**Flamingo Cafe.** *Caribbean.* Otherwise known as Rickie's, this little local hot spot offers limited local fare right on the beach beside Ocean Club Resort. It is more of a spot to grab a cold one in the middle of the afternoon or as the sun sets. You'll find many of the local residents catching

CLOSE UP

Groceries on Provo

If you have traveled throughout the Caribbean, you will have noted that grocery stores are not like they are at home. This is not the case on Provo. Not only is the Graceway IGA a North American–style supermarket—boasting a superb international section and excellent deli—but it rivals many you find across the United States, and is most definitely one of the best in the entire Caribbean. Located mid-island, it is a cab ride from the Grace Bay area. There is also the Gracebay Gourmet IGA just down from Seven Stars. In addition, the IGA has opened its third location downtown: $mart. It is another North American–style supermarket, but offers more to the locals at lower prices.

If you're shopping on a smaller scale, some resorts have small convenience stores for staples

such as milk, snacks, and coffee. The best, but by far the most expensive, is The Market at Blue Haven Resort in Leeward.

There is one main stop for alcohol other than in the three main IGA affiliates. The Wine Cellar, otherwise known as Discount Liquors, is on the south side of Leeward Highway between the roundabout at the top of Venetian Road and the roundabout at Suzy Turn.

One last mention is Provo's "red truck." Sitting on the left-hand side of the street as you enter downtown heading toward the airport is a lone red truck curbside. This is where residents pick up fresh fish caught by the little guy so they can avoid paying supermarket prices. You will find fresh catch of the day, as well as conch and lobster in season. This is a great stop for those with access to a grill.

---

up there, as the setting is terrific, with a porch to shade you from the sun and spectacular views of the beach. Island favorites include a curried grouper with coconut sauce that melts in your mouth, and tangy homemade barbecue ribs that are cooked on an open charcoal flame. You'll have to walk through the Cultural Center to get to the restaurant unless you come off the beach; you can do some light local shopping while you're there. ⑤ *Average main: $18* ⊠ *Cultural Center, Grace Bay Rd., Grace Bay* ☎ *649/242–7545* ✎ *flamingo_cafe@hotmail.com.*

$$$$ ✕ **Grace's Cottage.** *International.* This is considered one of the prettiest settings on Provo, and the name says it all. Imagine dining under the stars in an English-style garden or at one of the tables artfully set upon the graceful covered veranda skirting the gingerbread cottage. Tangy and exciting entrées include Saffron Seafood, vegetarian risotto, and the blackened chicken breast with tobacco onions. The portions are small, but the quality is high. You might want to end with the delicious chocolate soufflé. A nice touch is the small stool ladies are given so that their purses do not have to sit on the ground. On Tuesday night live music adds to the good vibes. ⑤ *Average main: $42* ✉ *Point Grace, Off Grace Bay Rd., Grace Bay* ☎ *649/946–5096* ⊕ *www.point grace.com* ⚓ *Reservations essential* ⊘ *No lunch.*

$$$ ✕**Grill Rouge at Grace Bay Club.** *International.* The Grill's setting, right on Grace Bay Beach, is simply lovely. Brightly covered umbrellas shade diners. Tables are set upon a wooden deck, with the menu more casual than that of Grace Bay's Infiniti. Typical fare includes a crab club sandwich and shrimp taco-tini, as well as a charred pork chop. Of course, you can try their conch salad if you want something a little more local. Tuesday is Caribbean Beach BBQ, and Saturday night is the seafood buffet. The Grill is open seven days a week for breakfast, lunch, and dinner. This is Grace Bay Club's family-friendly restaurant. Note that service can be slow; you are supposed to be relaxing! ⑤ *Average main: $30* ✉ *Villas at Grace Bay Club, Bonaventure Crescent, Grace Bay* ☎ *649/946–5050* ⊕ *www.gracebayclub.com.*

$$$$ ✕**Hemingway's.** *Eclectic.* The casual yet gorgeous setting, with a patio and deck offering unobstructed views of Grace Bay, makes this one of the most popular tourist restaurants. At lunch you can't miss with the soft grouper tacos or fish-and-chips. The mango shrimp salad is also excellent. For dinner there is a great kids' menu as well. Order the popular "Old Man and the Sea," which features the fresh fish of the day. If you're on a budget, go right before 6 pm, when you can still order from the less expensive lunch menu. Live music a couple of nights a week adds to the ambience. Ask when Brentford Handfield and his son take the stage. ⑤ *Average main: $32* ✉ *The Sands at Grace Bay, Grace Bay Rd., Grace Bay* ☎ *649/946–8408* ⊕ *www. hemingwaystci.com.*

$$$$ ✕**Infiniti.** *Eclectic.* Formerly known as Anacaona of Grace Bay Club, this chic palapa-style, open-air restaurant has the most romantic setting along Grace Bay, and for most, in all of the Turks and Caicos Islands. Despite its elite clientele and high prices, the restaurant continues to offer a memorable dining experience minus any formality or attitude, even though men are expected to wear long pants and collared shirts, and children under 12 are not allowed. Oil lamps create an evening glow, and the murmur of trade winds

adds to the Edenic ambience. Mesmerizing ocean views, along with exquisite service, make this an ideal choice when you want the best without a care in the world. The kitchen uses the island's bountiful seafood and fresh produce to craft superb cuisine. They also offer a raw bar, featuring a variety of ceviches: scallops, salmon, and mahimahi. It's a good thing the setting is amazing, as the portions are "elegantly" sized. ⑤ *Average main: $40* ⊠ *Grace Bay Club, Grace Bay Circle Rd., Grace Bay* ☎ *649/946–5050* ⊕ *www.gracebayresorts.com/gracebayclub* ⚓ *Reservations essential* ☷ *Closed Sept. No lunch*.

$$$$ ⨯ **Le Bouchon du Village.** *Bistro.* If you close your eyes, the aromas and flavors you'll experience at this bistro in Regent Village Plaza may make you think that you're sitting in a Parisian bistro. The food is exactly what you would expect, including escargots, foie gras, steak au poivre with frites, duck confit, and charcuterie and cheese boards, as well as superb fresh bread. Their many conch dishes and lobster salad add an island flair to the otherwise bistro chalkboard menu. A favorite for lunch is merguez sausage and frites, and the Chilean sea bass is a wonderful choice for dinner. Although reservations are not needed, this place is extremely popular with residents at dinner. The restaurant's chef, Pierrik, is the original owner of Caicos Cafe and had a loyal following for a reason. ⑤ *Average main: $34* ⊠ *Regent Village, Grace Bay Rd., Grace Bay* ☎ *649/946–5234* ☷ *Closed Sun.*

$$ ⨯ **LunaSea Pool Bar and Grill.** *American.* At the Somerset Resort you may enjoy lunch or dinner under shade in the sunken outdoor dining area or around one of several tables at the pool's edge, with views of the gorgeous colors of Grace Bay as your backdrop. You'll think you're truly having your burger in paradise. Other lunch offerings include a fabulous Mediterranean platter comprising grilled peppers, marinated olives, tabouleh, and tzatziki with grilled pita. The double-fried chicken wings with piri-piri ginger sauce are outstanding. For the pizza lover, there are several to choose from, as well as a panino or fish-and-chips. The bartender makes exotic tropical martinis, such as the mango-tini, that you can sip by the pool. The bar will even bring buckets of beer to you on the beach, so you never have to leave your little patch of sand. Ask about the Tuesday night Caribbean Beach Party, which includes a beach bonfire, music, and dancing. ⑤ *Average main: $15* ⊠ *The Somerset Resort on Grace Bay, Princess Dr., Grace Bay*

☎ *649/946–5900* ⊕ *www.thesomerset.com* ⚓ *Reservations not accepted* ☽ *No dinner.*

$$$$ ✕**Opus Wine-Bar-Grill.** *Eclectic.* A beautifully landscaped patio makes a quiet, elegant setting, or you may choose to eat in the air-conditioned dining room. You'll find a wide range of fish and meat on the menu. Try their lobster summer rolls with sweet chili dipping sauce or the spicy chili steak wraps with lemon hummus for a wonderful starter, followed by bone-in rib-eye with crumbled Gorgonzola. If you want fish, order one of the daily specials. And who can pass up caramelized pear with Gorgonzola? You can be sure of enjoying live music with local artists during the week. ⑤ *Average main: $32* ⊠ *Ocean Club, Grace Bay Rd., Grace Bay* ☎ *649/946–5885* ⊕ *oceanclubresorts.com/our-resorts/dining/opuswinebargrill* ☽ *No lunch. Closed Sun.*

$$$$ ✕**Parallel 23.** *Caribbean.* Dining at Parallel 23 is reminiscent of old-world charm. Tall French doors open onto the wide, elevated terrace overlooking a courtyard peppered with uplighted date palms, a fountain adding a quiet tinkle in the background. The international menu features a roasted beetroot carpaccio served on quinoa crackers, as well as the Angus beef duet: braised beef cheek and grilled fillet. There are also several gluten-free and vegetarian options. For dessert, try the lemon meringue pie drizzled with raspberry sauce and topped with fresh berries. This romantic spot is perfect for that extra-special evening, so dress up and enjoy! ⑤ *Average main: $41* ⊠ *Regent Palms Resort, Regent St., Grace Bay* ☎ *649/946–8666* ⊕ *www.regenthotels.com* ⚓ *Reservations essential* ☽ *No lunch.*

$$$$ ✕**The Pavilion at the Somerset.** *International.* Located at the Somerset Resort, dining may be at one of several tables elegantly set overlooking a formal garden courtyard. Indoors there is a different vibe altogether—cool and chic with high ceilings. It is one of Provo's few indoor, air-conditioned restaurants. The executive chef mixes international styles with Caribbean, Asian, and Europe flair. Some of the standouts are the herb-crusted rack of New Zealand lamb with chimichurri sauce and the pan-roasted Cornish hen. You could easily make a meal out of a couple of appetizers, including ceviches, too. End the meal with a slice of the triple-layer chocolate fudge cake. Ask for simpler off-the-menu options for the children. Justin, the chef, is also available for in-room chef service at the Somerset. ⑤ *Average main: $40* ⊠ *The Somerset, Princess Dr., Grace Bay* ☎ *649/946–5900* ⊕ *www.thesomerset.com.*

$$$ ✕ **The Plunge at Regent Palms.** *American.* Although oceanfront, The Plunge is deep set by the pool so that diners are out of the wind and can enjoy a relaxed meal. Alternatively, you may eat on the seaside deck. Both offer shade under full umbrellas. This is a casual dining option; beachwear is acceptable during the day, so no need to head up to your room to change—and visitors can stroll in right off the beach. The casual menu has nice lunch and dinner items. Enjoy a light lunch of Caesar salad with blackened shrimp or a spinach salad. You will find sandwiches, hamburgers, grilled meats, and fish. More upscale options are offered at dinnertime. ⑤ *Average main: $30* ✉ *Regent Palms, Regent St., Grace Bay* ☎ *649/946–8666* ⊕ *www.regenthotels.com.*

$ ✕ **The Pork Shack.** *American.* Believe it or not, this little guy has two locations. The title says it all. There is no name on the front of either building; the downtown location is simply a brown wooden shack, but you can ask anyone along Airport Road how to get there. It looks like someone's garden shed, but it serves the best chicken, pork, and steak sandwiches islandwide. The second location is in Alverna's Craft Market and serves a delicious Corona-battered cod fish-and-chips that is not to be missed. ⑤ *Average main: $8* ✉ *Alverna's Craft Market, Grace Bay* ☎ *649/232–1068.*

$$ ✕ **Seaside Café.** *American.* The casual restaurant at Ocean Club West is similar to the Cabana Bar & Grill at Ocean Club East. The usual casual fare, including hamburgers, salads, and wraps, can be eaten with a view of Grace Bay Beach, poolside, all day long and into the night. You can enjoy live music Monday, Wednesday, and Friday nights. This is a good spot for those days that you don't want to get dressed up but would rather kick back and relax. ⑤ *Average main: $15* ✉ *Ocean Club West, Grace Bay Rd., Grace Bay* ☎ *649/946–5880* ⊕ *www.oceanclubresorts.com.*

$$$$ ✕ **Seven.** *Caribbean.* Elegant and beautiful, this swanky restaurant at Seven Stars Resort is one of only a few on island with air-conditioning; there's also a covered patio with attractive outdoor seating that's ideal on pleasant evenings. Begin your evening with a beverage on The Deck, and then move over to experience innovative, artfully prepared food. You may choose to start with a favorite—roasted lobster bisque—followed by the beef tenderloin done with a potato rissole and a Cabernet reduction, or the tiger shrimp beggar's purse with its Asian influences. The lobster, among the best on the island, is served with a delicious rum-butter sauce when in season. Meals are served with a variety of flavorful salts from Salt Cay. ⑤ *Average*

main: $35 ⊠ *Seven Stars Resort, Grace Bay Rd., Grace Bay* ☎ *649/339–3777, 649/941–7777* ⊕ *www.sevenstarsgrace bay.com* ⊘ *Closed Sun.*

$$ ✕**Smokey's.** *Caribbean.* Smokey has been popular regardless of where he's been on the island, and he's sure been all over—he is an island legend! People flock for fantastic ribs and authentic "peas n' rice." He makes an amazing fried pot snapper, and his cracked conch is the island's best, making this one of the most popular local places to eat. The handy location is just above the Caicos Royale Casino, in Turtle Cove at the Queen Angel Resort. It's easy for tourists and locals to mingle—and perhaps play a game of slamming dominoes. Or try your hand in the nonsmoking casino downstairs. No need to look for a menu; just ask, "What's cooking?" ⑤ *Average main: $18* ⊠ *Queen Angel Resort, Turtle Cove* ☎ *649/946–4386* ⊟ *No credit cards.*

$$ ✕**The Thai Orchid Restaurant.** *Asian.* Within walking distance of numerous resorts and easier on the wallet than most other nearby restaurants in the heart of Grace Bay, this is a tiny little haunt, tucked neatly away in the Regent Village Plaza. You can dine in a relaxed, air-conditioned dining room or at one of the several tables along the sidewalk. They offer an amazing pad thai, probably one of the best you have tasted in the finest of Thai restaurants across North America. Their fried rice and curries are also delicious. A favorite is the crispy duck served on a bed of noodles with a garlic–and–sweet chili sauce. The menu is quite extensive, and everything is good. This is one way to get your Asian fix while visiting Provo. You can also ask for takeout. ⑤ *Average main: $20* ⊠ *Regent Village Plaza, Grace Bay* ☎ *649/946–4491* ⚹ *Reservations not accepted.*

$ ✕**Turks Kebab.** *Mediterranean.* A young Turkish man and his wife have set up shop in Alverna's Craft Market, just down from Gracebay Gourmet IGA. The Pita Doner Kebab is outstanding. This is truly authentic, and simply awesome. Locals often gather for a bite to eat and a beer. The menu is quite extensive, so there's something for everyone at an average of $12 per person. They also cater parties, so have them to your villa for a group gathering. Delivery is free with three or more orders in the Grace Bay area, but don't hesitate to enjoy the company of others in their funky little seating area right out front. ⑤ *Average main: $12* ⊠ *Alverna's Craft Market, Grace Bay* ☎ *649/431–9964.*

$$$ ✕**The Vix Bar & Grill.** *Eclectic.* The ambience at this upscale, outdoor café, which is in a pretty courtyard at Regent Village, is quite relaxed. Produce is fresh, burgers are certi-

fied dry-Angus, and seafood is local. Their chicken wings as an appetizer are great, but you can also try their tuna tartare. The Vix has several salads for those looking for lighter fare, as well as herb-crusted grouper. British pub fare is served on Thursday, and there is a kids' menu from $8 with the usual items: chicken tenders, penne pasta, and mini-burgers. Local expats often drop in late at night. ⑤ *Average main: $25* ⊠ *Regent Village, Regent St., Grace Bay* ☎ *649/941–4144* ⊕ *www.thevix.com.*

$$ ✕ **Yoshi's Sushi & Grill.** *Japanese.* Yoshi's offers excellent sushi in an indoor, air-conditioned setting or open-air on a lovely streetside patio. The menu here is reasonably priced by Provo's standards, but expect a much higher bill than you would find at your average sushi spot near home. Their menu includes a wide variety of sushi such as conch rolls, lobster rolls, and fresh game-fish sashimi, in addition to delicious specialties such as the Volcano, Mexican, and Caribbean. You will also find udon noodle soups, bento boxes, crispy fish salad, a chicken teriyaki—even steaks. ⑤ *Average main: $18* ⊠ *Saltmills Plaza, Grace Bay Rd., Grace Bay* ☎ *649/941–3374* ⊕ *www.yoshissushi.net* ⊘ *Closed Sun.*

THE BIGHT

$$$$ ✕ **Kitchen 218.** *Eclectic.* Relatively new on the scene, this restaurant is at the Beach House with the pool as its backdrop, simple and uncomplicated. A unique feature is their seven-course tasting menu with wine pairing. The regular menu features a nice tuna tartare, a pumpkin ravioli suitable for the vegetarian, and superb coconut-herb mahimahi, among many other fish dishes. This menu is expensive. An average appetizer is $20, and a lobster tail goes for $59. ⑤ *Average main: $40* ⊠ *The Beach House, Lower Bight Rd. 218, The Bight, N/A* ☎ *649/946–5800* ⊕ *www.beach housetci.com* ⚓ *Reservations essential.*

$$ ✕ **Somewhere Café and Lounge.** *Mexican.* This is a great location for a casual dining option—right on Grace Bay Beach overlooking tranquil waters. It is the perfect spot to enjoy midday, as bathing attire is perfectly acceptable, with Coral Gardens snorkeling only a few steps away. There's an adult-only bar/lounge on the upper deck, offering amazing views and full breeze. Much of the menu is made from scratch, with desserts prepared by residents and delivered daily. You will thoroughly enjoy the chips-and-salsa trio; the guac is to die for. All the regular Mexican dishes are there,

plus a super Tex-Mex breakfast. The portions are large. There's live music most nights, with a DJ on Sunday afternoons, making this a very lively spot. ⑤ *Average main: $18* ✉ *Coral Gardens Resort, Lower Bight Rd., Lower Bight* ☎ *649/941–8260* ⊕ *www.somewherecafeandlounge.com.*

★ Fodor'sChoice × **Stelle.** *Contemporary.* The setting is chic— **$$$$** some would even say swanky—with white fabrics blowing in the wind, diners dressed for clubbing, and tables surrounding a courtyard with views of the lighted pool. It's as if a small piece of South Beach has been transported to the tropics, albeit with an old-world flair. Even the food is chic; the menu changes often, so that Gansevoort groupies will always find something different and unique. It is a favorite of many. On Friday and Saturday nights you'll find the restaurant transformed into Provo's only high-end dance spot; a DJ plays music, with dancing picking up around 11 pm. For lunch, head to their beach bar called Zest—you don't even have to change out of your beach or pool attire. ⑤ *Average main: $40* ✉ *Gansevoort Turks + Caicos, Lower Bight Rd., Lower Bight* ☎ *649/946–5746, 786/558–5522* ⊕ *www.gansevoorthotelgroup.com.*

TURTLE COVE

$ × **Angela's Top o' the Cove New York Style Delicatessen.** *Deli.* Order a coffee, tea, bagel, deli sandwich, salad, and dessert at this island institution (opened in 1992) on Leeward Highway, just south of Turtle Cove. They also have great pizza, which you can order by the slice or by the box. There are tables in the air-conditioned indoor room, as well as on a shaded patio outside. The location's not close to where most tourists stay, but it's worth the drive. From the deli case you can also buy the fixings for a picnic; the shelves are stocked with a selection of fancier food items, as well as some beer and wine. They have a nice casual breakfast that starts at 6:30 am for early risers. ⑤ *Average main: $10* ✉ *Leeward Hwy., Turtle Cove* ☎ *649/946–4694* ⊕ *www. provo.net/topothecove* ⊘ *No dinner.*

$$$ × **Baci Ristorante.** *Italian.* Aromas redolent of the Mediterranean waft from the open kitchen as you enter this local favorite directly on Turtle Cove. Outdoor seating is on a lovely canal-front patio, or you may choose to dine at a table in the open-air, covered restaurant. The menu offers a small but varied selection of Italian dishes. Veal is prominent, but main courses also include pasta, chicken, fish, and excellent brick-oven pizzas. They have a lovely bruschetta, superb lasagna, and great seafood dishes. Their tiramisu is one of the best. The owner personally visits each and every table once guests are seated, going through specials and assisting you with your wine selection. ⑤ *Average main: $25* ✉ *Harbour Towne, Turtle Cove* ☎ 649/941–3044 ⊕ *baci-ristorante.com* ⊘ *Closed Sun. No lunch Sat.*

$ ×**Greenbean.** *Café.* Although most of the fancier restaurants on Provo are terrific, sometimes you just want to pick up something fast. Start the day with breakfast sandwiches and a variety of coffee choices. Even though Starbucks brand is brewed here, you can purchase the only locally roasted coffee on island by TCI Coffee Roasters. Daily specials, great panini, artisan flatbread pizzas, and fresh sandwiches are possibilities at Greenbean, as well as 50 available "toss-ins" for salads and wraps. It's a great choice for vegetarians. There's free Wi-Fi, and the restaurant also rents snorkel gear for off-the-beach snorkeling nearby. ⑤ *Average main: $12* ✉ *Harbour Towne, Unit 1, Turtle Cove* ☎ 649/941–2233 ⊕ *www.greenbeantci.com* ⊘ *No dinner.*

$$$$ ×**Magnolia Wine Bar and Restaurant.** *Eclectic.* The hands-on owners here, Gianni and Tracey Caporuscio, make success seem simple. Expect well-prepared, uncomplicated dishes. From their outstanding appetizers, try the chicken vegetable spring rolls or the roasted beets and fresh mozzarella. One of their top have-to-have mains would be the sesame-crusted rare seared tuna. Their Banoffee Pie or Vanilla Roasted Strawberries should end every meal. The bar deck's atmosphere is romantic, with only a few tables tucked off to the side. The adjoining wine bar includes a handpicked list of specialties that can be ordered by the glass. The hilltop setting is a great place to watch the sunset with the best views of Turtle Cove Marina. ⑤ *Average main: $30* ✉ *Miramar Resort, Lower Bight Rd., Turtle Cove* ☎ 649/941–5108 ⊕ *www.magnoliaprovo.com* ⌑ *Reservations essential* ⊘ *Closed Mon. No lunch.*

★   Fodor'sChoice ×**Sharkbites Bar & Grill.** *American.* At this casual
$$ local favorite the standard fare includes everything from the
FAMILY   local catch of the day, sandwiches, and island specialties to wings or nachos and beer along with other bar snacks. For those French Canadians visiting, they have a great poutine. It's a casual place for lunch—the deck overlooks Turtle Cove Marina, where you may be lucky enough to see sharks passing by. Friday-night happy hour is very popular, but don't take the table at the corner of the deck; several locals might get annoyed if you sit there! Live music makes this a very lively spot later on. For dinner there is an excellent almond-crusted grouper. You can expect to have

Lobster Night in season. Sit on the deck outside if you want to avoid the sports crowd enjoying the big-screen TVs that hang over the bar. They have a great souvenir T-shirt that you may want to purchase. ⑤ *Average main: $17* ⊠ *Turtle Cove Marina, Bridge Rd., Turtle Cove* ☎ 649/941–5090 ⚓ *Reservations not accepted.*

$$ ✕ **Tiki Hut.** *American.* From a location overlooking the

FAMILY marina, the ever-popular Tiki Hut serves consistently tasty, value-priced meals in a fun atmosphere. Locals take advantage of the Wednesday night chicken-and-rib special, and the lively bar is a good place to sample local Turk's Head brew. There's a special family-style menu, the best kids' menu on Provo. Don't miss pizzas made with the signature white sauce, or the jerk wings, coated in a secret barbecue sauce and then grilled—they're out of this world. The restaurant can be busy, with long waits for a table. It's part of a little drama on the island; 23 years ago they settled right on the water and then moved to a much larger location at the end of the marina. For you die-hard fans, they have moved "back to where it all began." However, it is bigger and better than ever. Doug, one of the longtime owners, has upscaled the operation since it last sat here, offering four different seating options: lounge-style closest to the water, a beer garden picnic-table deck for regular fare, undercover A-frame indoor dining, and Bamboo Room poolside dining. There's a fab beach volleyball court right next to the restaurant with a full-on bar, lighted at night, open for a game of two-on-two up to five a court. ⑤ *Average main: $20* ⊠ *Turtle Cove Marina, Suzy Turn, Turtle Cove* ☎ 649/941–5341 ⊕ *tikihut.tc.*

LEEWARD

$$$ ✕ **Fire & Ice.** *Eclectic.* This restaurant is exquisitely set at the Blue Haven Resort & Marina, with Leeward Channel and red mangroves as its backdrop. Start and end your evening with a drink in one of the waterside hammocks or lovely nooks set along the man-made spit overhanging the channel; the seating is comfortably arranged around a fire table, with glass to block the stronger breezes and cooler winds during the winter months. Dining can be under the stars or open air, under-roof. You'll find such entrées as grilled lobster, pork tenderloin, or the garden risotto with tofu for vegetarians. They also offer an amazing Chilean sea bass on pumpkin purée. For dessert there is a passion-fruit curd with cocoa crumble and berry compote. ⑤ *Average*

main: $30 ⊠ *Blue Haven Resort, Leeward* ☏ 649/946–9900
⊕ *www.bluehaventci.com* ⊘ *Closed Wed.*

$$ ✕**Salt.** *Eclectic.* This is the casual counterpart to Fire & Ice,
set off to the side from the resort at Blue Haven Marina,
again with views of Leeward Channel and the magnificent
yachts moored at the docks. It's very simple with a modern
edge. You will find bar bites, salads, and a few burgers and
sandwiches to choose from, as well as a selection of meats
and fish with a selection of sauces. This is a good spot to
head to after a day of diving or kayaking with Big Blue, as
it is right next door. And there is an outdoor pool table out
front as well as a sand volleyball court. ⑤ *Average main: $20*
⊠ *Blue Haven Marina, Leeward* ☏ 649/946–9900 ⊕ *www.
bluehaventci.com* ⚲ *Reservations not accepted.*

DOWNTOWN

$ ✕**Caribbean Cuisine.** *Indian.* This is a wonderful little spot
serving Guyanese Indian cuisine that is just down the road
from the airport. There is not a set menu, but rather a white
board where they jot down what's in the pot that day.
You are sure to find amazing rotis and curries, and they
always have something for the vegetarian, such as a dahl
or chickpea option to be enjoyed with homemade naan.
The delicious food just can't be beat. There are several
tables inside an air-conditioned space, or you can choose
the takeaway option. Either way, go early, because it closes
at 6 pm. ⑤ *Average main: $10* ⊠ *Airport Rd., Downtown*
☏ 649/242–3906 ⊘ *No dinner.*

$ ✕**Homey's.** *Caribbean.* This is a must-try, as it has deli-
cious home-style island cooking. They have a wide array
of local dishes and something for everyone. You don't eat
there, but there's a drive-thru for those coming off the
beach and just wanting to grab and go. For less than $10
you can order a full meal consisting of peas or okra and
rice, a barbecue main, and another side. Waters and soft
drinks are only $1, and the service is great. Try the nine
honey-mustard wings or their famous mac and cheese
with a peppery zip. ⑤ *Average main: $8* ⊠ *Leeward Hwy.,
Downtown* ☏ 649/941–5758.

DISCOVERY BAY

$ ✕**Mis Amigos.** *Mexican.* This quiet little Mexican restau-
rant is a bit out of the way, albeit centrally located right
on Leeward Highway. It's no-frills and barefoot-casual. A
sign over the door reads "This ain't Grace Bay." But the

food here is fantastic and the service down-home friendly. A residents' favorite is their buttermilk-fried-chicken burger with avocado and coleslaw. Beware, it's got a huge kick. Of course all the other regular Mexican items are on the menu, too. ⑤ *Average main: $12* ⊠ *Central Square, Leeward Hwy., Discovery Bay* ☎ 649/441–7314.

BLUE HILLS

★ Fodor'sChoice ✕ **Da Conch Shack.** *Caribbean.* An institution in
$$ Provo for many years, this brightly colored beach shack is justifiably famous for its conch and seafood. The conch is fished fresh out of the shallows and broiled, spiced, cracked, or fried to absolute perfection. This is the freshest conch anywhere on the island, as the staff collect it from their "pens" several times a day as needed. If you don't like seafood, there's also chicken. Their blackened grouper is to die for, and they actually have Johnny fries (french fries with a black bean and local pepper sauce). Give them a call to find out when they have theme nights or live music from 7 to 10 pm (Hump and Bump Night). Sunday afternoons you will listen to a live DJ from 1 to 5. You get to dine with your feet in the sand or on a wooden deck, right on the water's edge. ⑤ *Average main: $15* ⊠ *Blue Hills Rd., Blue Hills* ☎ 649/946–8877 ⊕ *www.conchshack.tc.*

$$ ✕ **Kalooki's.** *Caribbean.* This little restaurant is amazingly casual but also simply amazing, bragging a large wooden deck right on the beach in Blue Hills. This local spot serves the usual island fare, including fish fingers and fritters, burgers and jerk chicken. It's a good alternative to Da Conch Shack, which can be overwhelmingly busy at times. ⑤ *Average main: $18* ⊠ *Blue Hills Rd., Blue Hills* ☎ 649/339–1100 ⊕ *www.kalookisrestaurant.com.*

$$ ✕ **Three Queens.** *Caribbean.* Three generations have run the popular "locals" eatery—making it the oldest restaurant on the island—since long before there was ever a hotel or resort on Provo. Ms. Martha will tell you what's on the menu every day; always count on grouper and conch. Many a wonderful steak has also been had in this little haunt. There's always a game of slammin' dominoes going on, but what's best is the local gossip. Find out what's going on on both sides of the political table. Be forewarned, there is no glamour here. It is "down and dirty." This is also the hub of the annual Conch Festival held in November. ⑤ *Average main: $18* ⊠ *Blue Hills Rd., Wheeland, Blue Hills* ☎ 649/941–5984.

FIVE CAYS

$$ ✕**Bugaloo's.** *Caribbean.* Bugaloo's beach shack started the conch craze. The man behind the name started out in a wee little beach shack down in Wheeland many moons ago, moved to Freeport, came back, and has since opened up his newest location on the beach in Five Cays. Island attitude, with sayings such as "Ain't saying it had to been" and R-rated (or maybe X-rated) music, abounds. Of course, there's conch prepared many different ways, as fritters, cracked, salad, and so on. There's also fresh fish and fried chicken. On Sunday afternoon there's a "conch crawl" with live music, when rum punch flows a little more freely than normal and things can get quite lively. Located right next to the fisheries, this is even a little more local than Da Conch Shack, but keeping up the standards and service that visitors are looking for. This one is a must-do. Ⓢ *Average main: $14* ✉ *Five Cays Beach, five cays* ☎ *649/941–3863.*

CHALK SOUND

$$$ ✕**Las Brisas Restaurant & Bar.** *Eclectic.* With exquisite views
FAMILY of Chalk Sound, the setting here is deliriously lovely. The restaurant terrace deck and elevated gazebo offer picture-postcard views of the intensely blue waters of the sound. This is the only restaurant on Provo that offers an excellent authentic paella (if you order this, give it time—the flavors have to simmer). The menu also includes tapas, so you can enjoy a long lunch, indulging while you gaze at the gorgeous water. Dinner takes a little longer, as everything is made to order; you pick out your fish or meat, decide how you want it prepared, and choose a sauce for it. Try any one of their beef entrées, as they are all wonderful; their seafood creole is also great. If you want to experience the sound from the water, Las Brisas also has a cruising boat that holds up to 12 people. You can start your evening with a cruise at $50/person and ask for your predinner cocktails and appetizers to be served on board. Ⓢ *Average main: $25* ✉ *Neptune Villas, Chalk Sound Rd., Chalk Sound* ☎ *649/946–5306* ⊕ *www.neptunevillastci.com* ⊘ *Closed Tues.*

NORTHWEST POINT

★ Fodor'sChoice ✕**The Restaurant at Amanyara.** *Eclectic.* You'll
$$$$ be in awe as you walk through the stunning grand foyer of Amanyara into the open-air dining pavilion; you can sink into a cozy nook or choose from one of many teak

tables scattered under the shade of island mahogany trees or overlooking the lovely reflecting pools. But make sure to begin at the bar, with its high wooden ceiling a feat of engineering; all seating has dramatic sea views across the beauty of the lava rock–lined infinity-edge pool. The signature mojito is spectacular with its fresh mint, freshly ground sugarcane, and a shot of champagne. If it's a glass of wine you're looking for, they have a wide selection. The food is excellent, with the freshest seafood and choicest cuts of meat available on Provo. The menu changes daily, but always includes a good selection, so that all members in your dining party are happy. Their team behind the scenes will not disappoint you, but be sure to allow plenty of time for any Amanyara experience, as it is far more than just a meal. If you are not an Amanyara guest, you must make a call for special access privileges. Reservations must be made at least two days in advance for either lunch or dinner. ⑤ *Average main: $40* ⊠ *Amanyara Resort, Malcom's Road Beach, Northwest Point* ☎ *649/941–8133* ⚓ *Reservations essential.*

WHERE TO STAY

Providenciales has become an incredibly popular destination for a reason. No matter the budget, all accommodation meets what North Americans and Europeans consider acceptable standards. You will find the majority of hotels and resorts to be within the greater Grace Bay area, with a few in outlying areas taking advantage of their seclusion or unique beauty. Almost all are impeccably maintained; they are clean and comfortable, with up-to-date, modern conveniences such as air-conditioning, satellite TV, and Wi-Fi. Because Provo is relatively new to the tourism business by Caribbean standards, most accommodations are just a few years old. The majority of them are individually owned condos placed in a rental pool and treated as part of a resort. You get the best of both worlds in these condo resorts: consistency in style and standard of accommodation, and shared amenities that would not otherwise be possible, such as glamorous pools, spas, full gyms, and restaurant services. At the moment there are few hotel chains represented, but you will find the all-inclusive Club Med and Beaches resorts.

Most resorts on Provo are composed of privately owned condos that are placed into the resort's rental pool when the owners are not present. Unlike at chain hotels and resorts, you cannot request a particular building, floor, or room unless you are a repeat visitor. If you fall in love with the condo, you can probably purchase it or one that's similar. There are no taxes in Turks and Caicos except for a onetime stamp-duty tax—no property tax and no rental tax—which makes owning your own piece of paradise even more tempting.

Hotel reviews have been shortened. For full information, visit Fodors.com.

PRIVATE VILLAS

Provo is one of the better islands in the Caribbean for renting a private villa; there is a plethora to choose from that offer a clean, comfortable home away from home. Villas are scattered across the island, so you can choose whether you want to be close to activity or have peace and quiet. Rentals range from romantic one-bedroom cottages to fantastic multibedroom mansions on private stretches of beach—and everything in between. If you do stay in a villa, then it's most likely that you'll need to rent a car. Only a few are within proximity of restaurants. Some are in quiet residential neighborhoods, such as Leeward, where the homes may be on a canal, a couple of blocks from the beach. Several villas are in quiet Turtle Tail, quite centrally located and overlooking the beauty of the Caicos Banks. Many of those around Sapodilla Bay, Taylor Bay, and Chalk Sound have gorgeous views in all directions. A villa can offer a more budget-friendly vacation if you split the costs with other couples or families.

RENTAL AGENTS

Coldwell Banker TCI. Several agents at Coldwell Banker will assist you in selecting a property islandwide. ☎ 649/946–4969 ⊕ www.coldwellbankertci.com.

Prestigious Properties. Modest to magnificent condos and houses in the Leeward, Grace Bay, and Turtle Cove areas of Providenciales are available from this company ☎ 649/946–4379 ⊕ www.prestigiousproperties.com.

Seafeathers. Based in Providenciales, this locally owned and operated business specializes in Turtle Tail villa rentals. ✉ Turtle Tail ☎ 649/941–5703 ⊕ www.seafeathers.com.

T.C. Safari. Based in Florida, this company manages numerous properties around Provo. ☎ 649/941–5043, 904/491–1415 ⊕ www.tcsafari.tc.

TC Villas. Based in Atlanta, TC Villas has representatives to assist you in your villa selection. ☎404/467–4858 ⊕ *www. TCVillas.com.*

Turks and Caicos Reservations. They call themselves a "mini-Expedia" and are the official booking service on island. The staff can recommend a large inventory of resorts and select villas to those wishing to visit the islands. Everyone who books through the company receives travel rewards that go toward dinner vouchers, car rentals, or excursions, making repeat bookings an advantage. They will work hard to get you the best deal, book your flights, and act as concierge, and when there are storms or delays, they will help find emergency accommodations. ☎649/941–8988, 877/774–5486 ⊕ *turksandcaicosreservations.tc.*

CONCIERGE SERVICES

After 5 Island Concierge. Sometimes you just need help before or during your trip. After 5 Island Concierge can do everything from finding you a villa rental to providing grocery delivery. They will also help you arrange for a personal chef or catering service so that meals are not a concern during your condo or villa stay. Virtually any service you can think of can be arranged through this company. ☎649/232–3483, 649/231–0731, 877/404–9535 ⊕ *www.islandconciergetc. com.*

WHAT IT COSTS IN U.S. DOLLARS				
	$	**$$**	**$$$**	**$$$$**
Hotels	under $150	$150–$250	$251–$350	over $350

Hotel prices are per night for a double room in high season, excluding taxes, service charges, and meal plans (except at all-inclusives).

GRACE BAY

The vast majority of hotels and resorts on Providenciales are found along its beautiful north shore, between Turtle Cove Marina on the west and Leeward on the east, including world-famous Grace Bay.

$$$$ 🏝 **The Alexandra Resort.** *Resort.* This combined time share
FAMILY and condo resort is situated on a fine stretch of Grace Bay Beach, and is within walking distance of shops, snorkeling, and several excellent restaurants. ⑤ *Rooms from: $575* ✉ *Princess Dr., Grace Bay* ☎649/946–5807, 888/695–7591 ⊕ *www.alexandraresort.com* 🛏 *122 rooms* 🍽 *No meals.*

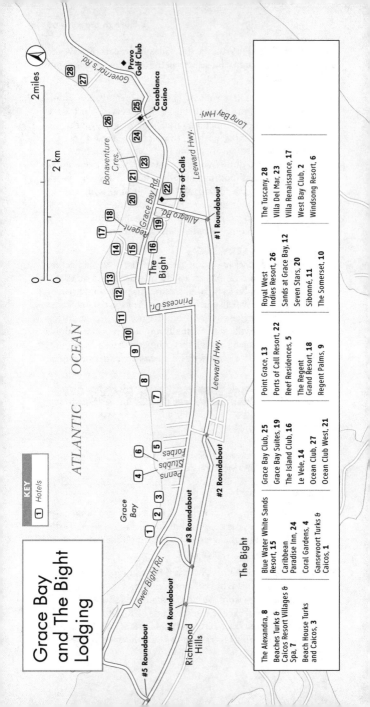

Grace Bay and The Bight Lodging

KEY
☐ Hotels

ATLANTIC OCEAN

Grace Bay

The Bight

Richmond Hills

The Bight

The Alexandra, 8
Beaches Turks &
Caicos Resort Villages &
Spa, 7
Beach House Turks
and Caicos, 3

Blue Water White Sands
Resort, 15
Caribbean
Paradise Inn, 24
Coral Gardens, 4
Gansevoort Turks &
Caicos, 1

Grace Bay Club, 25
Grace Bay Suites, 19
The Island Club, 16
Le Vele, 14
Ocean Club, 27
Ocean Club West, 21

Point Grace, 13
Ports of Call Resort, 22
Reef Residences, 5
The Regent
Grand Resort, 18
Regent Palms, 9

Royal West
Indies Resort, 26
Sands at Grace Bay, 12
Seven Stars, 20
Sibonné, 11
The Somerset, 10

The Tuscany, 28
Villa Del Mar, 23
Villa Renaissance, 17
West Bay Club, 2
Windsong Resort, 6

Provo
Golf Club

Casablanca
Casino

Governor's Rd.

Bonaventure Cres.

Grace Bay Rd.

Regent

Princess Dr.

Leeward Hwy.

Long Bay Hwy.

Allegro Rd.

Ports of Calls

Penns Stubbs Forbes

Lower Bight Rd.

#1 Roundabout
#2 Roundabout
#3 Roundabout
#4 Roundabout
#5 Roundabout

0   2 km
0   2 miles

2

★ Fodor'sChoice ⊡ **Beaches Turks & Caicos Resort Villages & Spa.** *All-*
$$$$ *Inclusive. Resort.* This property is the largest resort in the
FAMILY Turks and Caicos Islands by far. **Pros:** great place for families; all-inclusive; gorgeous pools; kids love this place. **Cons:**
with an all-inclusive plan you miss out on the island's other
great restaurants; excursions such as catamaran trip can get
crowded; very expensive; kids everywhere so not suitable
as a couples retreat. ⑤ *Rooms from: $770* ⊠ *Lower Bight
Rd., Grace Bay* ☎ *649/946–8000, 800/232-2437* ⊕ *www.
beaches.com* ⏎ *758 rooms and suites* ⦿ *All-inclusive.*

$$ ⊡ **Blue Water White Sands Resort.** *Rental.* This resort in the
middle of the hub offers easy access to nearby shops and
restaurants, and is within close walking distance of Grace
Bay Beach. **Pros:** very economical rates for Provo; great
management team with strong track record; close to night-
life, so no driving. **Cons:** with everything so convenient you
might not venture out to other areas of the island. ⑤ *Rooms
from: $159* ⊠ *382 Grace Bay Rd., Grace Bay* ☎ *649/432–
8633* ⊕ *www.bwwsresorts.com* ⏎ *12 suites* ⦿ *No meals.*

$$ ⊡ **Caribbean Paradise Inn.** *B&B/Inn.* Inland and about a
10-minute walk from Grace Bay Beach, this two-story inn
has terra-cotta walls and cobalt-blue trimmings. **Pros:** pay
a lot less by staying a block from the beach. **Cons:** front
desk not always manned; breakfast is extra. ⑤ *Rooms from:
$165* ⊠ *Grace Bay* ☎ *649/946–5020* ⊕ *www.caribbeanpara-
diseinn.com* ⏎ *18 rooms* ⦿ *Multiple meal plans.*

$$$$ ⊡ **Grace Bay Club.** *Resort.* This stylish resort retains a loyal
FAMILY following because of its helpful, attentive staff and unpretentious elegance. **Pros:** gorgeous pool and restaurant
lounge areas with outdoor couches, daybeds, and fire pits;
adult-only sections for those wishing a child-free vacation.
Cons: no children allowed at the Infiniti pool/restaurant,
although this can be a plus for many vacationers; have to
stay in Estates section to use its pool; expensive. ⑤ *Rooms
from: $630* ⊠ *Grace Bay Rd., behind Grace Bay Court,
Grace Bay* ☎ *649/946–5050, 800/946–5757* ⊕ *www.grace
bayclub.com* ⏎ *82 suites* ⦿ *Breakfast.*

$ ⊡ **Grace Bay Suites.** *Hotel.* Definitely rated as good value in
the Grace Bay area, this hotel is within a block of the beach.
Pros: you're only a block from the beach; some luxury for
less money. **Cons:** no views; not directly on the beach; no
stove in kitchenette. ⑤ *Rooms from: $145* ⊠ *Grace Bay Rd.,
Grace Bay* ☎ *649/941–7447* ⊕ *www.gracebaysuites.com*
⏎ *18 studios, 6 1-bedroom suites* ⦿ *No meals.*

$$$ ⊡ **The Island Club.** *Rental.* If you're on a budget, you will
find that this small condo complex gives you excellent

value. **Pros:** you can't get a better deal on Provo; centrally located, so you can walk everywhere; laundry facilities on-site; complimentary cell phones for each rental. **Cons:** only a few condos in the complex are in the short-term rental pool, so availability is limited; no phones in the room; a block from the beach; queen beds in the master bedroom. Ⓢ *Rooms from: $295* ✉ *Grace Bay Rd., Grace Bay* ☎ *649/946–5866* ⊕ *www.islandclubgracebay.com* ➴ *24 2-bedroom apartments* ⏐◯⏐ *No meals.*

$$$$ ⊡ **Le Vele.** *Hotel.* Modern and chic, this Italian-influenced condo complex with its minimalistic lines reminds one of a Miami South Beach hotel, minus the crowds. **Pros:** great central location; spacious rooms maximize the ocean views. **Cons:** residential feel isn't for everyone; the modern buildings don't blend with other resorts on the beach; pool is set back from beach without much ambience. Ⓢ *Rooms from: $395* ✉ *Grace Bay Rd., Grace Bay* ☎ *649/941–8800, 888/272-4406* ⊕ *www.levele.tc* ➴ *12 suites, 10 studios* ⏐◯⏐ *Breakfast.*

$$ ⊡ **Ocean Club.** *Resort.* Enormous, locally painted pictures
FAMILY of hibiscus make a striking first impression as you enter the reception area at one of the island's most well-established condominium resorts. **Pros:** family-friendly resort with shuttles between the two shared properties; screened balconies and porches allow a respite from incessant air-conditioning. **Cons:** although clean, furniture is dated; if you don't have a rental car, you have to take the shuttle to get closer to the "hub." Ⓢ *Rooms from: $229* ✉ *Grace Bay Rd., Grace Bay* ☎ *649/946–5880, 800/457–8787* ⊕ *www.oceanclubresorts.com* ➴ *174 suites* ⏐◯⏐ *No meals.*

$$$ ⊡ **Ocean Club West.** *Resort.* Its central location and affordable, comfortable rooms make this resort popular with vacationers. **Pros:** family-friendly resort with shuttles between the two shared properties; screened balconies and porches allow a respite from incessant air-conditioning; central location eases walking to shops and restaurants. **Cons:** rooms are a little dated; higher price point than Ocean Club. Ⓢ *Rooms from: $329* ✉ *Grace Bay Rd., Grace Bay* ☎ *649/946–5880* ⊕ *oceanclubresorts.com/ocean-club-west-resort/* ➴ *88 suites* ⏐◯⏐ *No meals.*

$$$$ ⊡ **Point Grace.** *Resort.* Keeping history in mind, this resort was built with a turn-of-the-last-century British colonial feel; dark mahogany, granite, marble, and teak create a sense of warmth and comfort within each of the 33 luxurious one- to four-bedroom suites and penthouses. **Pros:** relaxing environment; beautiful pool. **Cons:** can be extremely quiet

(signs around the pool remind you). ⓢ *Rooms from: $499* ✉ *Grace Bay Rd., Grace Bay* ☎ 649/946–5096, 888/209-5582 ⊕ *www.pointgrace.com* ⤳ *26 suites, 10 cottage suites* ⊘ *Closed Sept.* ⭢❶ *Breakfast.*

$$ ⛌ **Ports of Call Resort.** *Hotel.* At the former Comfort Suites, which has been completely refurbished, vamped up, and rebranded by new management, being a block from the beach means serious savings for those who are willing to be more than a few steps away from Grace Bay. **Pros:** economical alternative to beachfront properties; walking distance to main hub; "attached" to shopping area with restaurants. **Cons:** room key must be inserted for electricity to work (no leaving lights on when going out); peak season standard rooms require two-night minimum (though more expensive deluxe rooms do not). ⓢ *Rooms from: $189* ✉ *11 Sandcastle Rd., behind Port of Call, Grace Bay* ☎ 649/946–8888 ⊕ *www.portsofcallresort.com* ⤳ *98 suites* ❶ *Breakfast.*

$$$$ ⛌ **The Regent Grand Resort.** *Resort.* The name says it all, this resort is simply grand. **Pros:** majestic architecture; central location within walking distance of numerous restaurants and shops, including its own upscale Regent Village. **Cons:** no restaurant here, although many options are nearby. ⓢ *Rooms from: $705* ✉ *Regent St., Grace Bay* ☎ 649/941–7770, 877/288-3206 ⊕ *www.TheRegentGrandResort.com* ⤳ *21 suites* ❶ *Breakfast.*

★ Fodor'sChoice ⛌ **Regent Palms.** *Resort.* High on luxury, the
$$$$ Regent Palms has consistently scored in the top 100 Hotels
FAMILY in the World. **Pros:** lively; one of the best spas in the Caribbean; lots of amenities. **Cons:** in the summer the sunken pool bar area can get a bit hot when the trade winds die; expensive. ⓢ *Rooms from: $1,300* ✉ *Princess Dr., Grace Bay* ☎ 649/946–8666, 866/630–5890 ⊕ *www.regentpalmstci.com* ⤳ *72 suites* ❶ *Breakfast.*

$$ ⛌ **Royal West Indies Resort.** *Resort.* With a contemporary take on colonial architecture and the outdoor feel of a botanical garden, this unpretentious resort on Grace Bay Beach has plenty of garden-view and beachfront studios and suites for moderate self-catering budgets. **Pros:** great bang for your buck; on one of the widest stretches of Grace Bay Beach. **Cons:** Club Med next door can be noisy; staying in a unit at the back of the resort is no different from staying at some of the off-the-beach properties because of the resort configuration. ⓢ *Rooms from: $245* ✉ *Bonaventure Crescent, Grace Bay* ☎ 649/946–5004, 800/332–4203 ⊕ *www.royalwestindies.com* ⤳ *115 suites* ❶ *No meals.*

CLOSE UP

Crazy for Conch

"Belongers," otherwise known as islanders, once relied on fishing as the mainstay of their economy—before the arrival of tourism in Turks and Caicos. They truly know the importance of conch, not only as the country's largest export, but also as an integral part of the local diet. Today things have changed ever so slightly; now every part of the conch, from shell to meat, is used. Every restaurant in the Turks and Caicos serves some type of conch, in a sandwich, salad, fritter, soup, or even sushi, and the beauty of its shell has made its way into jewelry design and homewares. The shells may also be purchased in their somewhat natural state, albeit buffed and polished, and taken home as

per regulation—two per person. Shells are also crushed and used as exfoliates in a few spas around the islands.

Visitors to the islands may dive for conch as part of a day out on the water, and then enjoy it in a local dish later in the day as part of a beach barbecue. Alternatively, they can find it in any of the local restaurants. Conch can also be found embedded in the walls built around the homes in Salt Cay, not only for a tropical look but also to keep cows and donkeys out of the yard.

The Conch Farm is the only commercial conch farm in the world, and a visit will show you how conch is raised and give you information about its many uses.

$$ 🏨 **Sands at Grace Bay.** *Resort.* Spacious gardens and wind-
FAMILY ing pools set the tone for one of Provo's most popular family-friendly resorts. You can expect friendly and helpful staff and excellent amenities, including a spa, a good-size fitness room, water sports, tennis, and basketball, as well as on-site dining at this 6-acre all-suite beachfront resort. **Pros:** one of the best places for families; central to shops and numerous restaurants; screened balconies and porches give an escape from incessant air-conditioning. **Cons:** the pool deck is dark wood, so keep your sandals or flip-flops handy; avoid courtyard rooms, which are not worth the price; restaurant is busy. ⑤ *Rooms from: $250* ⊠ *Grace Bay Rd., Grace Bay* ☎ *649/941–5199, 877/777–2637* ⊕ *www. thesandstc.com* ⤶ *114 suites* ⦿ *No meals.*

★ **Fodor's**Choice 🏨 **Seven Stars.** *Resort.* Fronting gorgeous Grace
$$$$ Bay Beach, the tallest property on the island also sets a high
FAMILY mark for luxury within its three buildings, a magnificent heated pool, and huge in-room bathrooms. **Pros:** beachside

location; lovely inside and out; walking distance to everything in Grace Bay; terrific deck bar by the beach. **Cons:** some find the giant scale of the resort too big for the rest of the island; higher density than all other resorts. §*Rooms from: $490* ⊠ *Grace Bay Rd., Grace Bay* ☎ *649/941–7777, 866/570–7777* ⊕ *www.sevenstarsgracebay.com* ⇨ *116 suites* ❖*Breakfast.*

$ ☷ **Sibonné Beach Hotel.** *Hotel.* Dwarfed by most of the nearby resorts, the smallest hotel on Grace Bay Beach has snug (by Provo's spacious standards) but pleasant rooms with Bermuda-style balconies and a tiny circular pool that's hardly used because the property is right on the beach. **Pros:** closest property to the beach; the island's best bargain directly on the beach. **Cons:** pool is small and dated; some rooms have a double bed. §*Rooms from: $125* ⊠ *Princess Dr., Grace Bay* ☎ *649/946–5547, 800/528–1905* ⊕ *www.sibonne.com* ⇨ *29 rooms, 1 apartment* ❖*No meals.*

$$$$ ☷ **The Somerset.** *Resort.* This luxury resort has the "wow" factor, starting with the architecture and ending in your luxuriously appointed suite. **Pros:** the most beautiful architecture on Provo; located in middle, so you can walk to snorkel and walk to shops. **Cons:** the cheapest rooms are not worth the dollar value—they can get noisy. §*Rooms from: $640* ⊠ *Princess Dr., Grace Bay* ☎ *649/339–5900, 888/386–8770* ⊕ *www.thesomerset.com* ⇨ *53 suites* ❖*Breakfast.*

$$$$ ☷ **The Tuscany.** *Rental.* This self-catering, quiet, upscale resort is the place for mature, independent travelers to unwind without the need for resort amenities. **Pros:** luxurious; all condos have ocean views; beautiful pool. **Cons:** no restaurant or "reception," and it's at the far end of the hub; very expensive for a self-catering resort; can feel like no one else is on the property. §*Rooms from: $550* ⊠ *Grace Bay Rd., Grace Bay* ☎ *649/941–4667, 866/359–6466* ⊕ *www.thetuscanyresort.com* ⇨ *30 condos* ❖*No meals.*

$$ ☷ **Villa Del Mar.** *Hotel.* This resort offers some tremendous features for the price, even though it is not directly on Grace Bay Beach. **Pros:** close to some of the best restaurants on the island; within walking distance of Casablanca Casino; a bargain for the luxury. **Cons:** no on-site restaurant; no views from most floors; not directly on the beach. §*Rooms from: $250* ⊠ *1 Crescent Dr., Grace Bay* ☎ *649/941–5160, 877/345–4890* ⊕ *www.yourvilladelmar.com* ⇨ *18 studios, 24 suites* ❖*Breakfast.*

$$$$ ☷ **Villa Renaissance.** *Rental.* Modeled after a Tuscan villa, this luxury property is self-catering and not a full-service resort. **Pros:** luxury for less; one of the prettiest courtyards

in Provo. **Cons:** not a full-service resort. ⑤ *Rooms from: $580* ✉ *Ventura Dr., Grace Bay* ☎ *649/941–4358* ⊕ *www. villarenaissanceturksandcaicos.com* ⤵ *9 suites* ⦿ *No meals.*

THE BIGHT

$$$$ ⛱ **Beach House Turks and Caicos.** *Hotel.* On the quieter, western end of Grace Bay, this intimate all-suites resort has a unique Caribbean air. **Pros:** lush grounds; on one of the best stretches of Grace Bay Beach; great snorkeling very close by off the beach; more playful vibe. **Cons:** small bathrooms. ⑤ *Rooms from: $580* ✉ *Lower Bight Rd. 218* ☎ *649/946–5800, 855/946–5800* ⊕ *www.beachhousetci. com* ⤵ *21 suites* ⦿ *Breakfast.*

$$ ⛱ **Coral Gardens.** *Rental.* The best off-the-beach snorkeling directly in front of Coral Gardens makes this resort and its large condo units a very popular spot. **Pros:** resort fronts the best off-the-beach snorkeling spot on Provo; spacious rooms all have ocean views. **Cons:** restaurant can get lively at night so be sure to choose a unit with distance between; car rental recommended to get to the best restaurants and shops on island; confusing management setup. ⑤ *Rooms from: $209* ✉ *Penn's Rd., Lower Bight* ☎ *649/941–5497 Coral Gardens on Grace Bay, 800/787-9115* ⊕ *www.Coral GardensonGraceBay.com* ⤵ *25 suites* ⦿ *No meals.*

★ **Fodor's**Choice ⛱ **Gansevoort Turks + Caicos.** *Resort.* South Beach
$$$$ Miami meets island time at this gorgeous resort with modern, chic furnishings and a minimalistic vibe. **Pros:** service is excellent; staff is eager to please; gorgeous heated pool and amazing rooms with unprecedented views; great ambience. **Cons:** since this is one of Provo's few nightlife venues, Friday nights can get a little lively; need transportation for shops and exploring. ⑤ *Rooms from: $475* ✉ *Lower Bight Rd., The Bight, Lower Bight* ☎ *649/941–7555* ⊕ *www. gansevoorttc.com* ⤵ *55 rooms, 34 suites, 4 penthouses* ⦿ *Breakfast.*

$$ ⛱ **Reef Residences.** *Rental.* A smaller, more intimate resort set just back off the beach within proximity of some of the best off-the-beach snorkeling, Reef is both economical and convenient. **Pros:** nice pool; spacious rooms; close to a great snorkeling reef. **Cons:** you have to walk through another resort to get to the beach; rental car is recommended to get around; resort structure gets a bit confusing with the overlap with Coral Gardens. ⑤ *Rooms from: $249* ✉ *Stubbs Rd., Lower Bight* ☎ *649/941–3713, 800/532–8536* ⊕ *www.*

reefresidence.com ↪ *24 suites at Reef Residences, 8 suites at Coral Gardens* ↻*No meals.*

$$$$ ⚏ **West Bay Club.** *Resort.* A prime location on a pristine stretch of Grace Bay Beach just steps away from the best off-the-beach snorkeling makes this luxury resort a top pick. **Pros:** all rooms have a beach view; amazing luxury for the price. **Cons:** you'll need transportation to go shopping and to get to the main hub. ⑤ *Rooms from: $550* ⊠ *Lower Bight Rd., The Bight, Lower Bight* ☎ *649/232–2227, 649/946–8550* ⊕ *www.thewestbayclub.com* ↪ *46 suites* ⊙*Breakfast.*

★ **Fodor'sChoice** ⚏ **Windsong Resort.** *Resort.* On a gorgeous beach
$$$$ lined with several appealing resorts, Windsong just has that good feel all around, one that simply makes you feel at home. **Pros:** pool is unique; huge, gorgeous bathrooms; oh-my-goodness amazing penthouse rooftop decks. **Cons:** studios have only a refrigerator and microwave; no actual restaurant on-site. ⑤ *Rooms from: $390* ⊠ *Stubbs Rd., Lower Bight* ☎ *649/941–7700, 800/946–3766* ⊕ *www.windsongresort.com* ↪ *16 studios, 30 suites* ⊙*No meals.*

TURTLE TAIL

$$$ ⚏ **Harbour Club Villas.** *Rental.* Although not on the beach,
FAMILY this small complex of villas is by the marina, making it a good base for scuba diving, bonefishing, or that quieter-style vacation. **Pros:** centrally located, so only a five-minute drive from Grace Bay; great value; great base for divers; personable and friendly hosts; immaculately clean. **Cons:** need a car to get around the island; have to drive to a beach ⑤ *Rooms from: $255* ⊠ *36 Turtle Tail Dr., Turtle Tail* ☎ *649/941–5748, 888/240–0447* ⊕ *www.harbourclubvillas.com* ↪ *6 villas* ⊙*No meals.*

TURTLE COVE

$$ ⚏ **La Vista Azul.** *Rental.* You can save money by staying slightly away from the beach without giving up comfort or location. **Pros:** space and high-end comfort for a fraction of the cost on Grace Bay; views from the rooms are gorgeous; free Wi-Fi. **Cons:** too many stairs (three flights up from lobby to reach the elevators); rental car or taxi needed to get to many of the popular restaurants and sights; parking lot is at elevator level. ⑤ *Rooms from: $250* ⊠ *Lower Bight Rd., Turtle Cove* ☎ *649/946–8522, 866/519–9618* ✉ *reservations@lvaresort.com* ⊕ *www.lavistaazulresorttci.com* ↪ *23 condos.*

What Is a Potcake?

Potcakes are indigenous dogs of the Bahamas and Turks and Caicos islands. Traditionally, these strays would be fed leftovers from the bottom of the pot, hence the name. Much is being done today to control the stray-dog population. The TCSPCA and Potcake Place are two agencies working to find homes for the puppies. You can do a good deed by adopting one of these gorgeous pups; they will have received all their shots and have all the paperwork required to take them into the United States or Canada.

Even if you don't adopt, you can help by volunteering to bring one back to its adopted family, found online. Clearing customs in the United States is surprisingly easy when you bring back a potcake! If that's just not possible, be sure to stop by Saltmills and adopt a dog for an hour or two; they will very much appreciate a walk on the beach and a bit of love. For more information on how you can help, check out the website for Potcake Place (⊕ *www. potcakeplace.com*).

$ ☒ **Turtle Cove Inn.** *B&B/Inn.* One of the first to be built on the island, this two-story inn is affordable and comfortable. **Pros:** very reasonable prices for Provo; nice marina views. **Cons:** older; not on the beach; requires a car to get groceries or for other shopping excursions; can be a bit noisy. ⑤ *Rooms from: $129* ✉ *Turtle Cove Marina, Turtle Cove* ☎ *649/946–4203, 888/495–6077* ⊕ *www.turtlecove inn.com* ⇱ *28 rooms, 2 suites* ⦿ *No meals.*

NORTHWEST POINT

★   Fodor'sChoice ☒ **Amanyara.** *Resort.* Secluded. **Pros:** deliriously
$$$$ wonderful architecture; fabulous restaurant; the best sunset location on Provo; unprecedented service; the best full-service secluded beach on Provo. **Cons:** isolated; far from restaurants, outside excursion companies, and other beaches. ⑤ *Rooms from: $1,650* ✉ *Northwest Point* ☎ *649/941–8133* ⊕ *www.amanresorts.com* ⇱ *38 one-bedroom pavilions, 20 villas* ⦿ *No meals.*

LEEWARD

$$ ☒ **The Atrium.** *Rental.* This resort offers modern luxury
FAMILY   with upscale furnishings, only a 10-minute walk from the far eastern end of Grace Bay. **Pros:** luxury for the money; beachfront setup is isolated with only beach strollers pass-

ing through; quiet neighborhood; amazing pool. **Cons:** rental car is recommended for access to all that Provo has to offer; studios have only kitchenettes. ⓢ *Rooms from: $185* ⊠ *Governor's Rd., Leeward* ☎ *649/333–0101, 888/592–7885* ⊕ *www.theatriumresorttci.com* ⮞ *38 suites* ⦿ *No meals.*

$$$ ⬚ **Blue Haven Resort and Marina.** *Resort.* High on luxury, Blue Haven is the only resort on the far eastern end of the island, overlooking the beauty of au naturel Mangrove Cay and the mega-yachts moored dockside. **Pros:** fabulous amenities; large yachts to look over at docks. **Cons:** on a canal, so there is a current. ⓢ *Rooms from: $350* ⊠ *Marina Rd., Leeward* ☎ *649/946–9900, 855/832–7667* ⊕ *www.blue haventci.com* ⮞ *16 rooms, 35 suites.*

CHALK SOUND

$$ ⬚ **Neptune Villas.** *Resort.* Although not on the beach, this wonderful complex of villas is the only resort-style accommodation on the magical waters of Chalk Sound National Park, with nearby Sapodilla and Taylor bays. **Pros:** quiet location on Chalk Sound; great value; fabulous restaurant on-site; personable and friendly hosts; immaculately clean. **Cons:** a car is highly recommended; have to drive to all other attractions, services, and main beaches. ⓢ *Rooms from: $250* ⊠ *533, Chalk Sound Rd., Chalk Sound* ☎ *649/331–4328* ⊕ *www.neptunevillastci.com* ⮞ *9 villas.*

SPORTS AND THE OUTDOORS

BIKING

Most hotels have bicycles available for guests, or you can rent one from an independent company. Within Grace Bay, stick to the sidewalks for safety and be extremely careful when leaving the hub; drivers don't pay much attention to bikes!

Caicos Cyclery. Affiliated with Island Water Sports, Caicos Cyclery rents two different types of bicycles: beach cruisers ($25 daily) meant for gentle street riding, and mountain bikes for slightly rougher wear and tear ($40 daily). Discounts apply on rentals of more than two days. Staff are happy to deliver to your private villa, starting at $20 depending on where they're headed. ⊠ *Salt Mills Plaza, Grace Bay* ☎ *649/941–7544* ⊕ *www.caicoscyclery.com.*

Caicos Wheels. Beach cruisers are available from Caicos Wheels at $22/day. ⊠ *Grace Bay Court, Grace Bay* ☎ *831/824–8687, 649/946–8302, 649/946–8457* ⊕ *www.caicoswheels.com.*

Island Water Sports. Although this company rents kayaks ($150 daily) and paddleboards ($100), they also rent two different types of bicycles: beach cruisers ($25 daily), and mountain bikes ($40 daily). Discounts apply on rentals of more than two days. Staff is happy to deliver to your private villa, starting at $20 depending on where they're headed. ⊠ *Venture House, Venture Rd., Grace Bay* ☎ *649/941–7544* ⊕ *caicoscyclery.com.*

Scooter Bob's. You can rent beach cruisers at Scooter Bob's for $15 for a 24-hour period, and they offer a very reasonable drop-off service at $15 anywhere on the island if you rent for five days or longer. ⊠ *Turtle Cove Marina, Turtle Cove* ☎ *649/946–4684* ⊕ *www.scooterbobstci.com.*

BOATING AND SAILING

Provo's calm, reef-protected seas combine with constant easterly trade winds for excellent boating conditions. Several companies offer charters with snorkeling stops, food and beverage service, and sunset vistas. Prices range from $80 per person for group trips (subject to passenger minimums) to $800 or more for private charters.

FAMILY **Beluga Sailboat.** Beluga offers private charters for two to eight passengers. Owner-operator Tim Ainley, otherwise known as Captain Tim, knows these waters: he's been sailing them for more than two decades now. This is true sailing, no motors allowed. Staff will pick you up and take you to the marina where the boat is moored, and then ferry you off for a day of magic, exploring the reef and the cays east of Provo. Their specialty is a romantic encounter; all trips begin at $800. ☎ *649/231–0372* ⊕ *www.sailbeluga.com.*

★ **Fodor's**Choice **Caicos Dream Tours.** Caicos Dream Tours offers several boating options, including one that has you diving for conch before lunch off a gorgeous beach. You may choose from two different excursions shared with others, starting at $89/person, or decide to charter a boat all to yourself for as many as 12 people, beginning at $1,100 for a half day. With seven boats in their fleet, this company is able to accommodate up to 150 guests at the same time, so wedding parties and conference groups have the option of enjoying a day out together; the maximum capacity on one boat is 40 guests. They also offer a bottom-fishing charter for up to six people for those die-hard fishermen traveling together. Note that Caicos Dream Tours is the only island excursion operator that offers a combo of bottom-fishing and snorkeling on the same charter; this one makes the whole family happy! ✉ *Alexandra Resort, Princess Dr., Grace Bay* ☎ *649/231–7274* ⊕ *www.caicosdreamtours.com.*

FAMILY Fodor'sChoice **Island Vibes.** Turks and Caicos born and raised,
★ the boys who own and operate Island Vibes make their excursions stand out. If conditions are right, they'll give you the opportunity to snorkel out over the wall, where the reef drops an amazing 3,000 feet. With a roof slide, diving board, and spacious bathroom on board, these fun excursions add just a little more excitement to your day. Join a group for the half-day snorkel at $89/person, or throw yourself into their full-day barbecue adventure that combines an amazing lunch set up under the shade of tall island pines with exploring small cays, snorkeling, conch diving, and just plain beach strolling. There is also the option of a sunset cruise seven days a week. ✉ *Turtle Cove Marina, Turtle Cove* ☎ *649/231–8423* ⊕ *www.islandvibestours.com.*

Kenard Cruises. This luxury private catamaran is first-class all the way, including a chef who can prepare gourmet meals, a 42-inch TV, air-conditioning, and Bose surround sound. It can be chartered for a half day or full day on a custom itinerary—so you'll feel like a celebrity! ☎ *649/232–3866* ⊕ *www.kenardcruises.com.*

Sail Provo. Very popular for private charters, Sail Provo also offers scheduled half-day, full-day, sunset, and dedicated snorkeling trips to those who don't mind sharing with other holidaymakers on 52- and 38-foot sailing catamarans. They also head out on starlit evening cruises to share the marine world's glowworm extravaganza; underwater creatures light up the sea's surface not long after sunset a few days after the full moon each month. Check out their website to peruse the wide variety of excursions they offer with a beach pickup right in front of your Grace Bay resort. ✉ *Leeward* ☎ *649/946–4783* ⊕ *www.sailprovo.com.*

Silver Deep. Silver Deep excursions include several half-day and full-day trip options. You can choose from all types of fishing, a dedicated snorkeling adventure, exploration of North and Middle Caicos, and the most popular: a Native Beach Barbecue. Their most unusual opportunity is their night-fishing private charter, just in case your days are too busy with naps and enjoying the beach. Other private charters may be arranged starting at $1,100; your itinerary may be personalized to include a multitude of activities, keeping all members in your group happy. ⊠ *Ocean Club West Plaza, Grace Bay Rd., Grace Bay* ☎ 649/946–5612 ⊕ *www.silverdeep.com.*

FAMILY Fodor'sChoice **Sun Charters.** The *Atabeyra,* operated by Sun ★ Charters, is a 70-foot schooner with a big wide belly. It's the residents' choice for special events, as it is by far the most family-friendly adventure. Kids can run around without too many worries about going overboard, and the boom overhead is strong enough for them to sit and survey the seascape—just as a pirate would have done. Although they are primarily known as a private charter service, they also offer an amazing sunset rum punch party and glow-worm excursions as their specialty, with a weekly Sail & Snorkel for individuals to join in on. This good ship is also perfect for larger groups who wish to sail together, accommodating 2 to 50 people. ⊠ *Blue Haven Marina, Leeward* ☎ 649/231–0624 ⊕ *www.suncharters.tc.*

Undersea Explorer. For sightseeing below the waves, try the *Undersea Explorer,* a semisubmarine operated by Caicos Tours out of Turtle Cove Marina. It's an ocean adventure that takes you into the underwater world without getting wet! Your one-hour tour of the reef is led by a knowledgeable captain and viewed through large windows below the surface on either side, all in air-conditioned comfort. It's the perfect trip for young and old alike. Your choice: the Mermaid Adventure, which is a theatrical voyage with a "surprise" spotting of Mermaid Bella along the way and a pirate captain making a guest appearance, or the Turtle Reef Explorer, which sticks strictly to the business of exploring the reef as an informative voyage. ⊠ *Turtle Cove Marina, Turtle Cove* ☎ 649/432–0006 ⊕ *www.caicostours. com* ☎ $60.

Water Play Provo. Right on the beach, Water Play Provo has kites, Windsurfers, stand-up paddleboards, and kayaks. You can take a lesson, join a guided tour, or rent the equipment for multiple days or by the week. This company has taken over Windsurfing Provo. ⊠ *Ocean Club, Grace Bay Rd., Grace Bay* ☎ 649/331–3122 ⊕ *www.waterplay provo.com.*

CLOSE UP

Giving Back

Although the Turks and Caicos Islands are an upscale destination, that doesn't mean the nation has no one in need. Here are some worthwhile organizations you can contribute to.

■ **Edward C Gartland Youth Centre.** This nonprofit organization helps empower the youth of TCI, offering a variety of programs outside school hours. ⊕ *Ecgyouthcentre.com.*

■ **Potcake Place.** This organization rescues stray puppies from around the islands. You can donate dog items that are hard to find on an island (such as toys and formula). You can also volunteer to be a courier to take puppies to their forever homes or "adopt" one for the day and take it to the beach. ⊕ *www.potcakeplace.com.*

■ **Provo Children's Home.** This organization takes in orphans and is always in need of some kind of contribution. Requested items and directions for how to make personal pledges can be viewed on their website at ⊕ *www.pch.tc.*

■ **TCSPCA.** Here the SPCA also helps rescue stray puppies and dogs that wander the streets and provides free spay and neuter clinics and educational symposiums. The TSPCA also hosts special projects; they are currently working at improving the horse and donkey compound on Grand Turk. Donations are also appreciated, whether in cash, in kind, or your own volunteer time. wtcspca.tc.

■ **The Red Cross.** The organization takes in donations that go toward local needs as well as to the international organization. ⊕ redcross.org.

■ **The Salvation Army.** You will find a thrift store in the Graceway IGA complex where you may drop off any clothing or household items to be sold, with the profits going toward deserving causes such as children's feeding programs, transportation of the elderly, disaster management, and many others. ⊕ salvationarmy.org.

■ **The TCI National Trust.** The Turks & Caicos National Trust helps with preservation throughout the islands, maintaining historical sites and wildlife park areas. ⊕ *National trust.tc.*

■ **Turks and Caicos Reef Fund.** Helping to improve the awareness and preservation of the nation's reefs, this organization has annual fund-raising events that you may support. ⊕ tcreef.org.

■ **The Turks & Caicos Rotary Club.** The Rotarians give back in many ways, including eye-testing for schoolkids and donations of dictionaries, as well as island cleanups. ⊕ *Rotary.tc.*

Wild One. Thrill-seekers will enjoy this 45-minute jetboat ride that combines 360-degree spins and heart-racing nose-offs in water as shallow as 9 inches. You may get wet, so be prepared! The boat is operated by Caicos Tours out of Blue Haven Marina. ✉ *Turtle Cove Marina, Turtle Cove* ☎ *649/431–9453* ⊕ *www.caicostours.com.*

DIVING AND SNORKELING

★ **Fodor's**Choice Scuba diving was the sport that drew visitors initially to the Turks and Caicos Islands in the 1970s; diving here today is considered among the best in the world. The reef and wall drop-offs thrive with bright, unbroken coral formations and lavish numbers of fish and marine life. Mimicking the idyllic climate, waters are warm all year, averaging 76°F to 78°F in winter and 82°F to 84°F in summer. With minimal rainfall and soil runoff, visibility is usually good and frequently superb, ranging from 60 feet to more than 150 feet. An extensive system of marine national parks and boat moorings, combined with an eco-conscious mind-set among dive operators, contributes to an uncommonly pristine underwater environment. It is not unusual to spot reef sharks on every dive or to swim with whales during their migratory period between January and the end of March. Turks and Caicos has a wide variety of coral to note.

Off Providenciales, dive sites are primarily along the north shore's barrier reef. Most sites can be reached in anywhere from 10 minutes to 1½ hours. Dive sites feature spur-and-groove coral formations atop a coral-covered slope. Popular stops such as **Aquarium, Pinnacles,** and **Grouper Hole** have large schools of fish, turtles, nurse sharks, and gray reef sharks. From the south side, dive boats go to **French Cay, West Caicos, Southwest Reef,** and **Northwest Point.** Known for typically calm conditions and clear water, the West Caicos Marine National Park is a favorite stop. The area has dramatic walls and marine life, including sharks, eagle rays, and octopus, with large stands of pillar coral and huge barrel sponges.

Dive operators on Provo more regularly visit sites off **Grace Bay** and **Pine Cay** and make the longer journey to **Northwest Point** and **West Caicos,** depending on weather conditions. All major dive companies offer open-water dive and other certifications. You will even find technical diving, including re-breathers and Nitrox, available on island. Night diving is also available on the closer dive sites. A two-tank dive will range from $90 to $220. All companies offer gear rental at an additional fee. There are also two live-aboard dive boats available for charter working out of Provo.

Caicos Adventures. Run by the well-known and friendly Frenchman Fifi Kunz, Caicos Adventures offers daily trips to West Caicos, French Cay, and Southwest Reef off the south side of Provo. The company runs two dive boats, with groups up to 20 diving together. They also have the *Lady K*, a luxury motorboat available for private charters operating out of Blue Haven Marina. ✉ *Regent Village, Grace Bay Rd., Grace Bay* ☎ *649/941–3346* ⊕ *www.caicos adventures.com.*

Dive Provo. Dive Provo is a PADI five-star operation that runs daily one- and two-tank dives to popular Grace Bay sites as well as to West Caicos. In addition, they have their unique three-tank Scuba Safari, where they head out to some of the sites farther afield, such as Molasses Reef, Sandbore Channel, and Southwest Reef. This excursion includes one tank of Nitrox to make it easier on the diver to spend as much time as possible under the water. It is not offered to junior divers. ✉ *Ports of Call, Grace Bay Rd., Grace Bay* ☎ *649/946–5040, 800/234–7768* ⊕ *www. diveprovo.com.*

Provo Turtle Divers. Provo Turtle Divers, with its office at Ocean Club East, has been operating dive trips on Provo since the 1970s. The staff is friendly, knowledgeable, and unpretentious. They operate solely out of Southside Marina off Venetian Road. This location makes their boat trips quicker to the less traveled sites off French Cay, West Caicos, Northwest Point, and Sandbore Channel. Their years of experience make diving with them like spending the day with friends. ✉ *Southside Marina, Turtle Tail* ☎ *649/946–4232, 800/833–1341* ⊕ *www.provoturtledivers.com.*

Snuba Turks & Caicos. Snuba offers the next-best thing to diving for a noncertified diver; it's a very different experience from snorkeling, but requires no experience. With the Surface Nexus Underwater Breathing Apparatus, you go underwater amongst the coral and schools of fish like a scuba diver, but your air tank stays on a raft at the surface. It's a great way to experience the sport, giving you the opportunity to get a feel for it so that you might decide to take the full course and become certified at a later date. Children must be at least eight years old to participate.

Using the catamaran *Snuba Doo,* trips include a two-site day; one location focuses on the snuba experience, and the other offers a chance to do some more adventurous snorkeling out on the less frequently visited reefs off the Grace Bay Barrier Reef. Year-round off-the-beach snuba takes place on the reef right in front of Coral Gardens. Private charters are available for groups of up to 28. And note that the owner, Jodi Taylor, will take a picture of you underwater as a keepsake. ⊠ *Turtle Cove Marina, Lower Bight* ☎ *649/333–7333* ⊕ *www.snubaturksandcaicos.com.*

Turks & Caicos Aggressor II. The Turks & Caicos *Aggressor II,* a live-aboard dive boat, plies the waters throughout the islands, enjoying numerous pristine dive sites; weekly charters are out of Turtle Cove Marina. The *Aggressor II* has nine air-conditioned staterooms, all with TVs and DVD players, plus communal sundecks, wet bars, and hot tubs to keep you spoiled while on the water. You're met on arrival at the Providenciales International Airport and taken directly to the ship. Rates include up to five dives daily, plus all meals and beverages, including local beers and wine. ☎ *800/348–2628* ⊕ *www.aggressor.com.*

FISHING

The fertile waters around Turks and Caicos are great for angling—anything from bottom- and reef-fishing (most likely to produce plenty of bites and a large catch) to bone-fishing and deep-sea fishing (among the finest in the Caribbean). Several tournaments annually attract anglers from across the islands and around the world—with a significant number of Americans on the roster—who compete to catch the biggest Atlantic blue marlin, tuna, or wahoo. For any fishing activity, you are required to purchase a $15 visitor's fishing license; operators generally furnish all equipment, drinks, and snacks. Prices start at around $800 for a half day and go up from there, depending on the length of trip and size of boat. Outside of the following list of deep-sea operators, *see Boating and Sailing above* for operators who may take you out reef-, bottom-, and bonefishing.

Bite Me Fishing Charters. For deep-sea sportfishing, Captain Fineline does not require anyone to have previous experience, just a desire to get out on the water and enjoy the day. He has spent his entire life fishing the waters of TCI, and there isn't any local captain with more experience or more passion for his sport. *Hallelujah* is a 28-foot Blackfin with a 300-hp inboard motor. ✉ *Turtle Cove* ☎ *649/231–4420* ⊕ *www.turks-caicos-fishing.com.*

Grand Slam Fishing Charters. For deep-sea fishing trips in search of marlin, sailfish, wahoo, tuna, barracuda, and shark, look up this company. Grand Slam operates three boats: a 45-foot Hatteras, a 42-foot Pursuit, and a 28-foot WorldCat. ✉ *Turtle Cove Marina, Turtle Cove* ☎ *649/231–4420* ⊕ *www.gsfishing.com.*

Panoply Sportfishing & Charters. *Panoply,* owned and operated by residents of TCI for more than 25 years, is a 46-foot Bertram Sport Fisherman that charters deep-sea fishing trips, boasting a soft interior and state-of-the-art electronics. ✉ *Blue Haven Marina, Slip A19, Leeward* ☎ *649/432–3566* ⊕ *www.panoply.tc.*

Silver Deep. Silver Deep has been operating out of Provo for more than 25 years. In the fishing department, they offer deep-sea, bone-, and bottom-fishing. Families can choose to participate in a private excursion where fishing, beach time, and snorkeling can all be included to keep every member content. The company has 15 boats in which they work. ✉ *Ocean Club West Plaza, Grace Bay* ☎ *649/946–5612* ⊕ *www.silverdeep.com.*

FITNESS

Retreat Yoga & Wellness Studio. This is a studio for physical, mental, and spiritual development through the practice of yoga, tai chi, and holistic nutrition. Laura and Lindsay also offer nutrition consultations and wellness workshops. A raw juice bar and healthful snacks are offered on-site. ✉ *Ports of Call, upper floor, Grace Bay* ☎ *649/432–2485.*

GOLF

Golfing in the Caribbean can be quite an experience. The Provo Golf and Country Club has one of the finest layouts in the islands. Along with its smallish greens, the course is well manicured. If you forget your clubs, don't worry; you can rent a set that will accommodate your game. After a challenging round be sure to grab a drink or quick bite in the clubhouse that overlooks the 18th green. Usually, flamingos are spotted at the fifth green. Bring your "A" game, as this is truly a shot-maker's course.

★ ~~Fodor's~~ Choice **Provo Golf and Country Club.** Among the Caribbean's top courses, the 18 holes here (par 72) are a combination of lush greens and fairways, rugged limestone
outcroppings, and freshwater lakes. Fees are $160 for 18
holes with shared cart. The club also rents tennis equipment for use on its two lighted courts, which are among the
island's best. Nonmembers can play until 5 pm for $10 per
hour (reservation required). ⊠ *Governor's Rd., Grace Bay*
☎ *649/946–5991, 877/218–9124* ⊕ *www.provogolfclub.*
com 💲 *$160 for 18 holes, $85 for 9 holes with shared cart*
🏌 *18 holes, 6705 yards, par 72.*

HELICOPTER TOURS

TCI Helicopters. This is a very special way of seeing the
islands. Tours range from a quick trip around Provo for
20 minutes to 2.5 hours, during which you'll be whisked
all the way to Salt Cay and back again, taking in the full
string of islands. Their most popular tour is the 30-minute
tour of the cays; you'll have a good aerial view of Provo
and then head down the north shore of all the little cays
between the hub and Parrot Cay. The rate per person is
$245 with a minimum of two booking and a maximum
of four. Their charter rate where you can design your own
adventure is $1,400/hour. ⊠ *Williams Plaza, Downtown*
☎ *649/432-4354* ⊕ *www.tcihelicopters.tc.*

HORSEBACK RIDING

FAMILY **Provo Ponies.** Provo Ponies offers morning and afternoon
rides for all levels. Rides take you along quiet dirt roads,
through short brush trails, and then out onto Long Bay
Beach, where you and your horse may take a dip in the
shallow waters of the Caicos Banks before heading back to
the stable. A 60-minute ride costs $96; a 90-minute ride is
$118. Reservations are required, and there is a 200-pound
weight limit. You can get a pickup at your Grace Bay hotel
or villa (Grace Bay area only) for an additional $10 per
person, which is a good deal if you don't have a rental car.
It's closed on weekends, as the horses need a rest. ⊠ *Dolphin*
Rd., Long Bay ☎ *649/946–5252, 649/241–6350* ⊕ *www.*
provoponies.com.

PADDLEBOARDING

Stand-up paddleboarding is one of the fastest-growing sports in the Caribbean. Check out the following option if you wish to partake while on Provo:

Neptune Villas. You can rent paddleboards and kayaks at Neptune Villas to explore the magical waters of Chalk Sound National Park. On-site is also a superb restaurant overlooking the sound, Las Brisas, so you can enjoy a nice lunch after your independent excursion. ⊠ *Neptune Villas, Chalk Sound Rd., Chalk Sound* ☎ *649/331–4328* ⊕ *www. neptunevillastci.*

PARASAILING

Captain Marvin's Watersports. A 15-minute parasailing flight over Grace Bay is offered for just $85 (single) or $170 (tandem) from Captain Marvin's Watersports, which includes hotel pickup in the cost of your flight—within the Grace Bay area. This is not just for thrill-seekers, as the views from as high up as 450 feet give you a good understanding of how the Caicos cays are slung across the water between Provo and North Caicos. It also gives you spectacular views of the barrier reef that are truly unforgettable. You can also take a nonflyer along for the boat ride at $25. ☎ *649/231–0643* ⊕ *www.captainmarvinswatersports.com/.*

SkyPilot Parasail. You'll know you've spotted their sails when you see the bright orange one flying overhead, a large smiley face front and center. Here's another bird's-eye view that simply can't be beat, but you're not so high that you miss out on the larger marine life passing far below in the crystal-clear waters of Grace Bay. ☎ *649/333–3000* ⊕ *www. skypilotparasail.com.*

TENNIS

You can rent tennis equipment at the Provo Golf and Country Club and play on the two lighted courts, which are among the island's best.

Graceway Sports Centre. A full sports center with other activities available, Graceway has four newly built tennis courts to which visitors have access for $20/hour per court. Each court is equipped for cool, more refreshing night play, with hours from 9 am to 8 pm. There is also a tennis pro on-site if you would like to take advantage of your vacation time for a lesson or two. You will find the center right behind the main Graceway IGA supermarket. ⊠ *Grace Bay* 🕾 *649/442–6348.*

Provo Golf and Country Club. You can rent tennis equipment at Provo Golf and Country Club and play on the two recently refurbished hard-surface, lighted courts, which are among the island's best. Nonmembers can play until 5 pm for $10 per hour. Court times are from 7:30 am until 8:30 pm; reservations are required. ⊠ *Governor's Rd., Grace Bay* 🕾 *649/946–5991, 877/218–9124* ⊕ *www. provogolfclub.com.*

TOURS

Big Blue Unlimited. This ecotour operator got its start offering diving trips, but it has since branched out. Big Blue has several educational kayak ecotours to choose from. The very popular stand-up paddleboard (SUP) safari tours are an alternative, though they don't cover quite as much territory as the kayak tours. Big Blue also has outposts on all the Caicos Islands, with an extensive network of guides, bikes, kayaks, and boats, so they are able to recommend a number of interactive ecotourism excursions for those wishing to learn more about what Turks and Caicos has to offer. They also offer private charters with a maximum of 12 passengers, including snorkeling adventures to the barrier reefs on the outer islands along the Caicos Banks such as French Cay and West Caicos. They are perhaps best known for their kiteboarding and kitesurfing instruction, downwinders, and kite safaris. The Cabrinha Kite and Board gear is used for both instruction and rentals. ⊠ *Leeward Marina, Marina Rd., Leeward* 🕾 *649/946–5034* ⊕ *www.bigblueunlimited.com.*

Concha Woncha Tours. For a different tour of the island, let the air-conditioned turquoise trolley be your guide. The tour includes a visit to the Conch Farm and Chalk Sound National Park, a cultural show experience, and a full lunch at Da Conch Shack. Also included are all your beverages during the tour: water, nonalcoholic fruit punch, and a rum punch with a kick. Tours last three to four hours and are available on Monday, Wednesday, and Friday with a 10-person minimum. The trolley can also be chartered for special events. The tour ($119/adult) includes pickup and drop-off at your hotel or condo within the Grace Bay area. 🕾 *649/231–5665* ⊕ *conchawonchatours.com* ☉ *Tours Mon., Wed., and Fri.* ☉ *Closed Sept.*

Froggie's Ultimate Tours. From this location in Blue Hills, adventurous individuals may head off into the more rugged end of Providenciales on their very own ATV. Small groups are led along winding roads, on tracks cut through the brush, and down pristine natural beaches on the northwest end of the island to discover a side of Provo you could not otherwise get to know—all while having loads of fun. There's a small eatery where you "saddle up" and can grab a bite before or after your adventure, or pick up a cold drink to enjoy along the way. Note that you must be 18 years of age with a valid form of identification to rent the ATV, but only 12 years old to ride. ⊠ *Wheeland end of Blue Hills Rd., Blue Hills* ☎ *649/232–3764, 231–0595* ⊕ *froggiesatv.com.*

Paradise Scooters. New Vespa tours have arrived on Provo, where riders are guided throughout various island neighborhoods with stops along the way at the Conch Farm, Blue Hills, Sapodilla Bay, and Chalk Sound; a full lunch at Bugaloo's in Five Cays is included. Tours cost $146. The company also rents scooters starting at $30/day for a single rider, as well as hybrid electric bicycles. ⊠ *Grace Bay Plaza, Grace Bay Rd., Grace Bay* ☎ *649/333–3333* ⊕ *www. paradisescooters.tc.*

WATERSKIING AND WAKEBOARDING

Nautique Sports. Nautique Sports offers a water-sports dream: a range of activities from wakeboarding to waterskiing, wakesurfing, barefoot waterskiing, slalom waterskiing, wakeskating, tubing, and snorkeling. What better place to learn than on the calm, crystal-clear waters of Providenciales. A great company for beginners, Nautique offers private instruction and will have you skiing in no time. Experts can even try barefoot skiing—in the summer months. ⊠ *Near Blue Haven Marina, Leeward* ☎ *649/431–7544, 649/431–3566* ⊕ *www.nautiquesports.com.*

WINDSURFING

Although the water appears calm, the breezes always blow along Provo's northern shore. Most resorts will provide Windsurfers. If you're on Grace Bay Beach, stay inside the white buoys; boats can pass by beyond them. Nautique Sports also rents kite-surfing equipment *(see Waterskiing, above).*

FAMILY **SURFside Ocean Academy.** SURFside is the only scuba outfit in TCI to offer mobile scuba services and will bring the lesson to *you*! Why leave your private villa when you can have the adventure brought to your pool and oceanfront? SURFside also offers PADI's Discover Scuba Diver Program, their most popular scuba course, for individuals who are not yet certified but would like to try scuba diving, for ages 10 and up. In addition to scuba, the company provides custom charter cruises for smaller groups (maximum of eight passengers) on a private 20-foot Edgewater. The boat includes a tow arch for wakeboarders and water-skiers and stops for a custom barbecue lunch at the more remote and uninhabited islands like French Cay and West Caicos. You can also spend the day on the beach with provided chairs, umbrellas, and even coolers. SURFside is also well known for their stand-up paddleboard (SUP) experiences, and offers a variety of classes and tours, as well as an hour-long PaddleFit Fitness boot camp–style class and SUP "yoga on the water." ✉ *Grace Bay Club, Grace Bay* ☎ *649/231–5437* ⊕ *www.surfsideoceanacademy.com.*

FAMILY **TC Kiteboarding.** This is a small and friendly kiteboarding company that offers lessons from beginner through advanced, as well as providing kite rentals and repairs. You can find their office by heading out to Long Bay Beach, right next door to the Shore Club; they are under the black flag with a large white TCK emblazoned on it . . . unless they're out on the water. All TCK's gear is by Slingshot. This company is definitely teen friendly. ✉ *Long Bay Beach (next door to the Shore Club), Long Bay* ☎ *649/442–2423* ⊕ *www.tckiteboarding.com.*

SHOPPING AND SPAS

Provo is not really a shopping destination, and you won't find bargains here. However, there is enough upscale shopping to keep your wallet busy, from tropical clothes and jewelry to art prints and accessories. The shopping complexes in the Grace Bay area continue to expand, and the major resorts have small boutiques with signature items, so don't forget to check them out.

Local Souvenirs

What should you bring home after a fabulous vacation in the Turks and Caicos? Here are a few suggestions, some of which are free!

If you're a beachcomber, you might find a sand dollar or conch shells to bring home. But remember, much of the north shore is part of the Princess Alexandra National Park, so you are not allowed to take any-thing away —only enjoy it while you are there. You will have to go shelling outside the parks. Of course, you can find wonder-fully polished shells at many of the souvenir stops, as well as at the Conch Shack and Bugaloo's.

You'll find locally made ceram-ics at Art Provo, as well as at Turks & Caicos National Trust in Town Center Mall downtown.

There are two cultural centers, one between Ocean Club and Club Med next to Ricki's, and the other across the street

from Beaches' easternmost entrance. In addition, there is a crafts market called Alverna's Market on Dolphin Road, just down from Gracebay Gourmet IGA. Here you'll find a wide variety of items, including batik clothing, locally made jewelry, Haitian metal art, and much more. Custom-made pieces can be ordered.

One of the best souvenirs is the hardcover coffee-table cook-book from the Red Cross. Not only is it gorgeous, featuring recipes from all the wonderful chefs of the Turks and Caicos, but the proceeds help the Red Cross in its endeavors.

The best free souvenir—be-sides your phenomenal tan—is a potcake puppy. The puppy you adopt comes with carrier, papers, and all the shots—and will remind you year after year of your terrific vacation. Let's not forget there are local potkit-tens, too!

SHOPS

SHOPPING AREAS

There are several main shopping areas in the Grace Bay area: **Saltmills**, **La Petite Place**, and **Regent Village**, as well as **Ports of Call** Shopping Village. There are also two cultural centers, one between Ocean Club and Club Med next to Ricki's, and the other across the street from Beaches' east-ernmost entrance. Handwoven straw baskets and hats, polished conch-shell crafts, paintings, wood carvings, model sailboats, handmade dolls, and metalwork are crafts native to the islands and nearby Haiti. The natural surroundings have inspired local and international artists to paint, sculpt, print, craft, and photograph; most of their creations are on sale in Providenciales.

GRACE BAY

ARTS AND CRAFTS GALLERIES

★ Fodor'sChoice **Anna's and Anna's Too.** Anna's sells original artworks, silk-screen paintings, sculptures, and handmade seaglass jewelry, most made by local artists and artisans. It's a trove of fabulous finds! You won't leave without picking up a little something to take home with you. Her newest edition is Anna's Too, just a couple of doors down. This wonderful shop is filled with fantastic women's wear—all cotton, comfortable, and colorful. Tucked alongside are books and pillows as well as other home decor items. ✉ *Saltmills Plaza, Grace Bay* ☎ *649/941–8841.*

ArtProvo. This is the island's largest gallery of designer wall art, but native crafts, jewelry, handblown glass, candles, and other gift items are also available. Featured artists include Trevor Morgan from Salt Cay, and Dwight Outten. This is another spot where you are sure to find something to take home with you. ✉ *Regent Village, Regent St., Grace Bay* ☎ *649/941–4545* ⊕ *www.artprovo.tc.*

Driftwood Studio. You'll find fine arts, textiles, photography, and crafts in this new gallery on Provo that prides itself on bringing local art to its clientele. ✉ *Caicos Cafe Plaza, Grace Bay* ☎ *649/342–3052* ⊕ *driftwoodtci.com.*

Making Waves Art Studio. Sara, the owner and resident artist, paints turquoise scenes, often on wood that doesn't require framing. She is happy to discuss the possibility of transforming your thoughts and emotions about one special spot onto canvas as the perfect thing to take home. You'll find artists working on-site. Come and enjoy meeting these beasts in their natural habitats. They don't mind being fed! And bring wine! ✉ *F104, Regent Village, Grace Bay* ☎ *649/242–9588* ⊕ *www.makingwavesart.com.*

CLOTHING

Blue Surf Shop. This is the only true surf shop on the island. Affiliated with Big Blue Unlimited, they carry gear from such companies as Quicksilver, Billabong, Rip Curl, Roxy, Element, and Dakine. They are also the only ones that carry this country's very own ConchTCI wear. In addition, you will find polarized sunglasses from Oakley, Ray-Ban, SunCloud, and Von Zipper; a biodegradable sunscreen that does not affect what swims in the sea; and GoPro cameras, as they are the only licensed provider. Blue also carries an excellent selection of sandals—something that is hard to find, believe it or not—as well as snorkel gear. ⊠ *Salt Mills, Grace Bay* ☎ *649-/941–8670.*

Caicos Wear Boutique. This store is filled with casual resort wear, including Caribbean-print shirts, swimsuits from Brazil, sandals, beach jewelry, and gifts. On the more practical side of things, snorkel gear, inflatable beach toys, and towels might be something you need while visiting the island; you'll find them here. ⊠ *Regent Village, Grace Bay Rd., Grace Bay* ☎ *649/941–3346.*

Hidden Treasures Boutique. Ladies, this is the perfect little shop in which to find an elegant yet casual outfit for warm-weather wear. Hidden Treasures features international brands such as Saint Grace, Goddis, TBags, Yosi Samra, and Vitamin A swimwear. You will also find lightweight lingerie and undergarments, along with a small selection of accessories to complete the ensemble. Call ahead, as their hours are more limited than those of many other shops in Salt Mills. ⊠ *#9 Salt Mills Plaza, Grace Bay* ☎ *649/941–7425.*

Island Sportique. Island Sportique has been an important presence on Provo for many, many years now, providing the island with one of the only options for the purchase of sporting goods. They carry such brands as Adidas, Reebok, Nike, New Balance, Sperry, Speedo, and many more. You will find a limited range of running and tennis shoes, but also accessories for all sports, including tennis, basketball, squash, swimming, Pilates, and yoga. ⊠ *Regent Village, Grace Bay* ☎ *649/946–5378* ⊕ *www.islandsportique.com.*

FOOD

Grocery shopping in Provo is almost as good as at home, with all the American, British, and Canadian brands you crave. Because everything has to be flown in, expect to pay up to 50% more than for similar purchases in the United States. Even many hard-to-find products and special dietary foods can be found on Provo. Shipments come in on Sunday, so Monday is your best food-shopping bet.

Beer is expensive; rum is cheaper. Stores are prohibited by law from selling alcohol on Sunday. Although it's tempting to bring in your own cooler of food, remember that some airlines charge for checked bags, and there is the risk of losing luggage. More than likely, if it's allowed in the States, it's allowed on Provo—meat, fish, and vegetables can be brought in if frozen and vacuum-sealed; always ask your airline if you will be allowed to check a cooler. If you're traveling for more than a week, then you may save enough money by bringing provisions in with you to make it worth your while. But remember, if you're staying on Provo, there will be no problem buying anything you need.

Cuban Crafters Cigars. This company brings in Cuban tobacco and skillfully assembles a variety of cigars on Providenciales. They do this to bring the product to you at a more economical price. They also have a small selection of spirits to offer. ☒ *Saltmills, Grace Bay* ☎ *649/946-4600, 649/441–2823.*

FOTTAC. Flavors of the Turks and Caicos carries such specialties as local Bambarra rum and the spices and sauces that are made with it, rum cake, Turk's Head beer, local T-shirts, wineglasses, mugs, and locally made products. ☒ *Regent Village, Regent St., Grace Bay* ☎ *649/946–4081* ⊕ *www.bambarrarum.com.*

Graceway Gourmet. The Grace Bay branch of Provo's largest supermarket is likely to have what you're looking for, including a selection of nice wines and beers. It's walkable from many of the resorts, as it's right in the hub. It's especially popular for its prepared foods, which can be taken back and quickly reheated in your condo's kitchen when you don't feel like cooking from scratch or heading out to eat. You'll also find it's a good stop for inexpensive beach toys; there's a separate little corner for them just inside the door. ☒ *Dolphin Ave., Grace Bay* ☎ *649/333–5000* ⊕ *www. gracewaygourmet.com.*

★ Fodor'sChoice **Kissing Fish Catering Co.** Kissing Fish Catering Co. has the same owners as Bay Bistro. The company will cater events like full-moon bonfires on the beach, weddings, and private parties, including beachside romantic dinners for two. Choose options from pig roasts and ribs to four-course meals with grilled lobster, grouper with mango chutney, or jerk chicken and tasty salads, just to name a few choices from their extensive menu. If you're staying in a villa or condo with full kitchen, you can hire a personal chef to prepare meals in-house. Check out their website for dates of full-moon beach parties that you and your family won't want to miss. ☒ *Sibonné Beach Hotel, Grace Bay Rd., at Bay Bistro, Grace Bay* ☎ *649/941–8917* ⊕ *www.kissingfish.tc.*

JEWELRY

Jai's. Jai's is the place to go if you'd like to purchase a piece of luxury jewelry as a reminder of that special vacation. You will find names such as David Yurman, Doves, Gucci, Movado, Cartier, and Rolex, along with less expensive options, including their Pandora collection. If jewelry is not what you're after, they also carry a wide range of fragrances and sunglasses to choose from. With 20 years of experience serving Turks and Caicos, they know what you want. You'll also find them in the departure lounge at the airport. ⊠ *Regent Village, Regent St., Grace Bay* ☎ *649/941–4324* ⊕ *www.jais.tc.*

Rumeurs. What more could one mix into one little gem of a shop? But then there's a good chance you'll find something interesting to take home with you. Rumeurs has a wide assortment of items under one roof: jewelry, women's clothing, small pieces of art and sculptures, lighting, household items, and furniture—all with an Asian influence. ⊠ *Caicos Cafe Plaza, Grace Bay* ☎ *649/941–5569.*

SOUVENIRS

Caribbean Outpost. The Outpost, in the Regent Village Plaza, is an enormous souvenir shop, connected directly to the Goldsmith duty-free jewelry shop. You'll find such things as T-shirts, hats, beach cover-ups, beach towels and toys, sunscreen, Reef sandals, and so, so much more. This is not a quick stop to get in and out of. ⊠ *Regent Village, Grace Bay* ☎ *649/941–5599.*

Mama's Gift Shop. Mama's is the place for the usual souvenirs and trinkets. She has a great selection of T-shirts and hats, as well as shot glasses and fridge magnets. What really makes shopping fun is Mama herself; she makes everyone who walks through her door feel like family. ⊠ *Ports of Call Shopping Center, Grace Bay Rd., Grace Bay* ☎ *649/946–5538.*

TURTLE COVE

LIQUOR

Wine Cellar. Visit this store for its large selection of duty-free spirits, wine, and beer. ⊠ *1025 Leeward Hwy., east of Suzie Turn Rd.* ☎ *649/946–4536* ⊕ *www.winecellar.tc* ⊙ *Mon.–Sat. 8–6.*

Flamingos on Provo

Have you always wanted to see flamingos in their natural habitat? If so, then the Turks and Caicos is your place. On Provo the best place to see them up close is at the golf course, though to do so you have to play a round of golf. But across the island they are often spotted only a stone's throw away. Behind the IGA supermarket on Leeward Highway is Flamingo Pond, a popular feeding ground; to get there you must drive all the way down Venetian Road out to Turtle Tail. Beware: they're not always there, and the road is very rough. North Caicos has its own Flamingo Pond, with a small deck lookout, but you'll need binoculars to get a good look. And just across the causeway to Middle Caicos you'll stand a good chance of sighting flamingos up close if the weather is favorable.

DISCOVERY BAY

BOOKS

FAMILY **Unicorn Bookstore.** This is the place to go to supplement your beach-reading stock or if you're looking for island-specific materials. Unicorn has a wide assortment of books and magazines, including guides to the Turks and Caicos Islands and the Caribbean. There is also a large children's section with crafts, games, and art supplies. If you want to be sure to find your selection there, be sure to call ahead, as they will order it in for you. ⊠ *Leeward Hwy., in front of Graceway IGA* ☎ *649/941–5458* ⊕ *www.unicornbookstore.com.*

FOOD

Graceway IGA. With a large fresh-produce section, bakery, gourmet deli, and extensive meat counter, Provo's largest supermarket will have what you're looking for. The most consistently well-stocked store on the island carries known brands from the United Kingdom and North America, as well as a good selection of other international foods, and prepared items such as a great rotisserie chicken and pizza. Expect prices to be much higher than at home. This supermarket is one of the reasons why visitors come back to TCI again and again. They know they will find everything they choose back home—and then some. ⊠ *Leeward Hwy.* ☎ *649/941–5000* ⊕ *www.gracewayiga.com.*

Quality Supermarket. When the IGA is out of stock, this fairly typical small-town-style grocery store can sometimes fill the gaps. ⊠ *Hospital Rd.*

LEEWARD

FOOD

★ Fodor's Choice **The Market.** The Market prides itself on offering high-end gourmet and organic items, including a wide selection of fresh produce, international items, gourmet coffees and teas, dry goods, wine, beer, and spirits, as well as a range of smoothies and juices. While you're there, check out their café-style deli. You can grab a quick bite to eat and then pick up your shopping while enjoying a wonderful cappuccino. This is much more than convenience for those staying in the Leeward area. It's also the perfect spot for picking up specialty items that you may not find anywhere else on the island and where you can create a lovely picnic to take out on a boat trip leaving from right in front of The Market's door. ⊠ *Blue Haven Resort, The Boathouse, Leeward* ☎ *649/946–9900.*

CLOTHING

Undercover. Just in case your suitcase has gone missing, you'll be able to find a selection of undergarments and nightgowns in Undercover, conveniently located off Leeward Highway in Graceway Plaza. It's really the only place on the island to satisfy those needs. Both men and women will find what they need here. ⊠ *Graceway House, Leeward* ☎ *649/941–5911.*

DOWNTOWN

FOOD

$mart. The IGA has opened its third location downtown: $mart. It is another North American–style supermarket but offers more to locals at lower prices. You can cut your travel budget considerably by purchasing essentials, their reduced items, and lower-priced soft drinks and dairy products, as well as more reasonably priced meats, fruits, and vegetables. ⊠ *Town Centre Mall, Downtown.*

JEWELRY

Royal Jewels. This chain sells gold and luxury-brand jewelry, designer watches, perfumes, fine leather goods, and cameras—all duty-free. The main store is on Leeward Highway close to downtown, but they do have another location in Saltmills that is more convenient for guests staying in the Grace Bay hub. ⊠ *Leeward Hwy., Downtown* ☎ *649/946–4699.*

SOUVENIRS

Turks & Caicos National Trust. Buying locally made ceramics, straw hats and bags, and small wooden sailboats from the Trust's shop helps support the nation's historic sites and national parks. They also have a small selection of books. While visiting, be sure to ask any questions you may have about the various spots around the islands they watch over. ⊠ *Towne Centre Mall, Butterfield Sq., Downtown* ☎ *649/941–5710.*

SPAS

Provo is an amazing destination if you are looking forward to pampering yourself while on vacation. The spas here offer treatments with all the bells and whistles, and most get good word of mouth. Most of Provo's high-end resorts have spas, with access for those not staying on the property. There are also several independent spas to choose from, and for those staying in one of the many villas, there are services that also come to you.

Anani Spa at Grace Bay Club. Anani Spa at Grace Bay Club is on the Villas side of the complex. There are eight treatment rooms in total, but treatments can also be performed on your balcony if you're staying at Grace Bay Club, or in the spa tent on the oceanfront. Spa packages are available so that you can enjoy a combination of treatments designed to work together. One of their signature treatments is the Exotic Lime and Ginger Salt Glow; you will emerge refreshed and polished! ⊠ *Villas at Grace Bay Club, Bonaventure Crescent, Grace Bay* ☎ *649/946–5050* ⊕ *www.gracebayresorts.com.*

Beaches Red Lane Spa. One unique feature about this spa is that it has one hot plunge pool and one cold plunge pool. During special hours, it offers kids' treatments, too. Although Beaches is an all-inclusive resort, spa treatments are an additional charge to guests. The spa is also open to non-guests. ⊠ *Beaches Turks & Caicos Resort Villages & Spa, Lower Bight Rd., Grace Bay* ☎ *649/946–8000* ⊕ *www.beaches.com.*

Como Shambhala at Parrot Cay. Asian holistic treatments, yoga with the world's leading teachers in a stunning pavilion, and a signature health-conscious cuisine are all part of the program here. The infinity pool, Pilates studio, steam room, sauna, and outdoor Jacuzzi make you feel complete.

If you're staying on Provo, you can call for reservations, but you have to pay for the boat ride to Parrot Cay. Some consider this one of the finest spas in the world. In fact, visiting masters from "off island" are featured throughout the year. ✉ *Parrot Cay Resort, Parrot Cay* ☎ *649/946–7788* ⊕ *www.comoshambhala.com.*

Regent Spa. Widely considered one of the best spas in the Caribbean, the Regent Spa is an oasis of relaxation. In the main facility you will find a pedicure/manicure space, gym, boutique, and yoga and Pilates pavilion, as well as men's and women's steam rooms and saunas. Outdoors, white tented cabanas grace the edge of a beautiful reflecting pool, its waters catching images of towering palms and flowering bougainvillea. However, you don't even have to leave your room; massages may be arranged so that you can enjoy the wonderful sea views right from your very own balcony. Guests are encouraged to indulge in one of the locally inspired signature treatments: a mother-of-pearl body exfoliation incorporating the queen conch shell, or the 90-minute Zareeba herbal cleansing and detox. Rest a while and sip herbal tea or replenish with citrus-infused water before or after your treatment. ✉ *Regent Palms, Princess Dr., Grace Bay* ☎ *649/946–8666, 866/877–7256* ⊕ *www.regentpalmstci.com.*

Spa Sanay. Located at the Alexandra Resort, Spa Sanay offers facials, massages, body treatments, and nail services. There is also a line of men-only services, as well as on-site massages and hair and nail services where they come to you. ✉ *Alexandra Resort, Grace Bay Beach, Grace Bay* ☎ *649/432–1092, 649/946–5807* ⊕ *www.spasanay.com.*

Spa Tropique. You pick the place, and this spa comes to you—an ideal option for those in more isolated villas who can't bear to leave their island paradise. The spa can also come to your hotel room (provided your hotel has no spa of its own). Have your treatment on your balcony, or on the beach or by the pool, which will make it seem extra special. Spa Tropique's one-of-a-kind Turks Island salt glow incorporates local salts from Grand Turk and Salt Cay. The spa also has locations at Ports of Call, both Ocean Clubs, and the Sands Resort. ✉ *Grace Bay Rd., Grace Bay* ☎ *649/331–2400* ⊕ *www.spatropique.com.*

Teona Spa. Although the spa for the Regent Grand and Rennaisance, Teona has opened their second location at the Somerset. Both spaces exude a peace-filled ambience, with every detail carefully thought out. Hush as you enter, and relax while you're there. It is the spa choice for many island residents. Take a peek at the spa specials; there is always a combination package put together for special times of the year. Or try one of the spa parties. What better way to spend time with a young one than a Mommy and Me day? And if you wish to have your treatment in your own space, Teona will come to you. ✉ *The Regent Grand Resort, Regent St., Grace Bay* ☎ *649/941–5051* ⊕ *www. teonaspa.com.*

Thalasso Spa at Point Grace. Thalasso Spa at Point Grace offers their services from within three whitewashed open-air cabanas set upon the dunes overlooking Grace Bay. They share the European philosophy of the famous Thalgo Spas of France and combine it with the perfect Caribbean ambience for your enjoyment. Treatments combine elements of the ocean, including sea mud, seaweed, and sea salt, with the properties of seawater to pamper you from head to toe. The setting alone, with the salt air and sea breezes, is worth the visit. This is another favorite with residents. ✉ *Point Grace Resort, Grace Bay Rd., Grace Bay* ☎ *649/946–5096* ⊕ *www.pointgrace.com.*

NIGHTLIFE

Although Provo is not known for its nightlife, there are some live bands and bars. Popular singers such as Brentford Handfield, Just, Corey Forbes, and Quinton Dean are island boys who perform at numerous restaurants and barbecue bonfires. Be sure to ask if any ripsaw bands—aka rake n' scrape—are playing while you're on island; this is one of the quintessential local music types that is found more often on the family islands.

The best late-night action can be found at the Gansevoort Turks + Caicos, where DJs play until the wee hours on Friday night, as well as at either of the two main casinos, where everyone ends the night. If you want to see a show and dance until late, Club Med offers a night pass, which includes drinks. You'll also find a couple of songsters, including Sally Greenwood, at the Amanyara in the evening if you have decided to treat yourself to a very special night out.

Most restaurants and bars have happy hour every night. Check out Pelican Bay; they have a 50% off all drinks special from 5 to 7 every night of the week. It's a local's choice. You can take in the fish fry on Thursday night at the far end of Grace Bay, followed by some karaoke at Danny Buoys. Somewhere on the Beach is perfect for a Friday if you want to stay on the water; they have a local band play until late. On the upper end of the scale, locals enjoy a mellower evening at The Deck in Seven Stars, as well as Infiniti Bar at Grace Bay Club. If you have dined a bit later than you might have expected, you can grab a late-night drink at the SandBar, right across the street from Saltmills Plaza, or head on a bit of a road trip to Club 809. This is a Dominican bar just past Walkin Marine Supplies on the road heading out to Blue Hills; they have a pool table outside as well as dominoes, and a DJ with dancing on the inside. Chance Casino is downstairs. The rowdier crowd can also be found at Jimmy's Dive Bar.

Keep abreast of events and specials by checking **TCI eNews** (⊕ *www.tcienews.com*) or **WhereWhenHow** (⊕ *www.where-whenhow.com*).

FULL-MOON PARTIES. Full moons are reputed to make people a little crazy, so full-moon parties can be a lot of fun! Bay Bistro organizes a pig roast with tropical fare such as pineapple coleslaw alongside a bonfire several times a year when the moon is high. Give them a call to see if the month when you're visiting is one of the lucky ones. The evening is a great hit with all ages, even the kids, who can roast marshmallows and make s'mores while running crazy in the moonlight.

RECOMMENDED BARS

Danny Buoy's. A popular Irish pub, Danny Buoy's has pool tables, darts, and big-screen TVs. It's a great place to watch sports broadcasts from all over. Different nights feature different nightlife; Tuesday is karaoke, and other nights have live music. It's open late every night. Currently it's a hot spot for a nightcap. ⊠ *Grace Bay Rd., across from Carpe Diem Residences, Grace Bay* ☎ *649/946–5921* ⊕ *www.dannybuoys.com*.

CASINOS

Caicos Royale Casino. This casino offers American roulette, blackjack, dice, three- and four-card poker, Punto Banco, Texas Hold'em, and slot machines. ✉ *Lower Bight Rd., Queen Angel, Turtle Cove* ☎ *649/941–5770* ⊕ *www.caicos royale.com.*

Casablanca Casino. The Casablanca Casino has brought slots, blackjack, American roulette, poker, and craps to Provo. Because it's open daily until 4 am, you can come late and make it your last stop for the night. There are complimentary drinks while playing and you can get a free shuttle ride by contacting the casino. ✉ *Grace Bay Rd., Grace Bay* ☎ *649/941–3737* ⊕ *www.casablanca.tc.*

THE CAICOS AND
THE CAYS

By Laura
Adzich-
Brander

TURKS AND CAICOS CONSISTS OF MORE THAN 40 islands, eight of which are inhabited. Few visitors venture out from the tourist hub of Provo, but when they do, they discover a whole other side to the islands. All the outlying cays are uninhabited with the exception of two, offering much for the adventurous explorer. Parrot Cay, once known as Pirate Cay and home to Anne Bonny and Mary Reid, is now a highly sought-after 1,000-acre luxurious private resort, whereas Pine Cay is home to the quiet and secluded Meridian Club as well as a number of residents looking for the simpler life. South, North, and Middle Caicos are laid-back and charming, offering a step back in time.

All the cays have something unique to offer, whether that be observing iguanas, hiking through bird sanctuaries, or sitting on a quiet beach watching whales go by. With the fringing reef keeping the waves at bay, there is also endless snorkeling. And then there's the beauty of East Caicos, uninhabited by humans, and populated by donkeys and flamingos. The highest point of land in the Turks and Caicos is on East Caicos, where there are cave systems and endless beaches to comb.

PLANNING

GETTING HERE AND AROUND

Many of the uninhabited cays can be explored on day trips out of Provo. Boat excursion companies offer small-group trips to several of them, and you can also charter your own trip. Although the smaller islands between Provo and North Caicos can be reached only by boat from Provo, there is a regularly scheduled ferry service between Provo and North Caicos; from there you can drive across a causeway to Middle Caicos, which takes only about 30 minutes from the ferry landing by car. South Caicos can also be reached by ferry, albeit a long and often bumpy ride, so many choose one of several daily flights.

HOTELS

Accommodations throughout the Caicos islands are generally simple yet comfortable. There are small hotels and a few privately owned villas scattered throughout, offering clean lodgings with air-conditioning and often satellite TV. At the other end of the spectrum is Pine Cay's Meridian Club, like a luxury camp with a clubby atmosphere. And

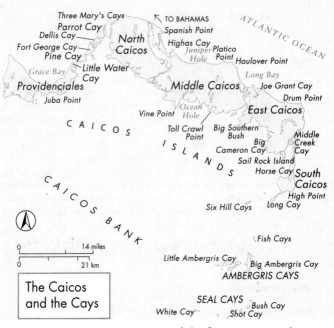

The Caicos and the Cays

then there's Parrot Cay, one of the finest resorts in the world. It is said that the highly anticipated Sailrock project will open its doors in 2016.

Hotel reviews have been shortened. For full information, visit Fodors.com.

RESTAURANTS

The outer islands don't offer much in the way of independent restaurants, and each island has only a handful of places to eat. Menus are often based on what was caught that day, which equates to wonderfully fresh fish, conch, and lobster dishes. It is always a good idea to call ahead. In fact, it is highly recommended that day-trippers take a small picnic with them, just in case the chef has decided to take the day off or everyone's at church. If you're staying at the Meridian Club on Pine Cay, meals are included in your room rate. Parrot Cay has two elegant and upscale restaurants. Both Parrot Cay and the Meridian Club are private resorts, but with advance reservations it's possible for nonguests to dine at both places. The excursion is very expensive, but many travelers find that it's worth it for the chance to visit.

PLANNING YOUR TIME

The smaller cays are all accessible only by boat, whether as part of an excursion or by private charter. A few may be reached by kayak for the more adventurous; check with Big Blue Unlimited, as their kayak rentals are closest to the cays between Provo and North. Both Parrot Cay and Meridian Club have private transportation from Provo for their own guests, whereas day-trippers must incur the transportation over at a cost. North Caicos and South Caicos are accessible by a very reliable ferry service operating out of Provo. Middle Caicos is connected to North Caicos by a causeway, so both of these islands can be visited in a single day, as can South Caicos if you're traveling by plane.

WHAT IT COSTS IN U.S. DOLLARS				
	$	$$	$$$	$$$$
Restaurants	under $12	$12–$20	$21–$30	over $30
Hotels	under $275	$275–$375	$376–$475	over $475

LITTLE WATER CAY

5 minutes by boat from Walkin or Leeward Marina.

This small, uninhabited cay is a protected area under the Turks & Caicos National Trust, and it's just a stone's throw away from Providenciales's Walkin and Leeward marinas. The trip over takes only 5 minutes from the Leeward end of the island, and an excursion boat out of Grace Bay takes 5 to 15 minutes. On these 150 acres are two trails, red mangroves, and an abundance of native plants. Boardwalks protect the ground, and interpretive signs explain the habitat.

The small island—known to many as Iguana Island—is home to about 2,000 rare, endangered rock iguanas. Although often described as shy, these creatures are actually quite curious. They waddle right up to you, as if posing for a picture. Please do not feed or touch the iguanas. They are wild animals.

Several water-sports operators from Provo and North Caicos include a stop on the island as a part of a snorkel or

TOP REASONS TO GO

Day excursions. All of Provo's excursion companies offer trips out to the cays. You can snorkel the reef, check out the iguanas at Little Water Cay, have a barbecue lunch on a secluded beach, and dive for conch all in one afternoon. On a full-day excursion you can go as far as Middle Caicos, where you can hike trails and explore caves. Keep an eye out for JoJo, the dolphin. He's the unofficial mascot of Turks and Caicos and may decide to join you on your trip.

Parrot Cay. Live like a rock star, if only for a day. Reservations are mandatory and not guaranteed, but if you can get here for lunch, it's oh-so worth it—extravagant, but worth every penny. Lunch guests get access to the gorgeous beach, pool, and one of the best spas in the world. It's definitely frowned upon for boats to moor off their beach; expect to be asked to leave, as their guests pay dearly for their privacy.

Pine Cay. If you need to forget your worries for a day, a week, or even longer, then this is spot for you. Call the Meridian Club to organize a boat transfer and head over for lunch. Everything here is rustic and charming, laid-back and relaxing, and the beach is one of the best.

3

sailing excursion. There's a $5 permit fee to visit the cay, and the proceeds go toward conservation in the islands.

GETTING HERE

The only way to reach Little Water Cay is by organized excursion or private boat (including kayak).

PINE CAY

15 to 20 minutes by boat from Provo.

Pine Cay's 2½-mile-long (4-km-long) beach is among the most beautiful in the archipelago. The 800-acre private island, which is in the string of small cays between Provo and North Caicos, is home to a secluded resort and almost 40 private residences. The beach alone is reason to stay here.

Nonguests of the Meridian Club can make reservations for lunch, and boat transfer can be arranged for an extra cost. Plan to spend the day enjoying the stunning beach, and be sure to ask what's on the day's menu since it changes daily. Saturday and Wednesday nights are buffet-style.

Saturday is also Jump-Up night, where the resort puts out their largest speakers and encourages everyone to "jump up and dance the night away!" On Wednesday, a quieter option, the kitchen staff pitches in to produce their favorite meals, making it the perfect time to try some local dishes.

GETTING HERE

The only way to reach Pine Cay is by private boat or on the Meridian Club's private service. Ask the resort to explain your transfer options, because the cost varies, depending on whether you take advantage of a shared boat or decide to organize a private trip (small boats cost $170 each way, larger boats cost $250 each way and up). You must make reservations, so don't count on making same-day arrangements.

WHERE TO STAY

★ Fodor'sChoice ⊺ **The Meridian Club, Turks & Caicos.** *Resort.* Feel-
$$$$ ing like a private club, this resort is on one of the most beautiful beaches in Turks and Caicos, and you can choose from the 12 oceanfront rooms, the one cottage, or one of the private homes around the island. **Pros:** the finest beach in Turks and Caicos; rates include some of the best food in the Turks and Caicos, as well as snorkeling trips. **Cons:** no TVs or phones, so you are really unplugged here; expensive to get back to Provo for shopping or other Provo-based excursions or activities; all this simplicity costs a great deal. ⑤ *Rooms from: $895* ✉ *North Shore* ☎ *649/946–7758, 866/746–3229, 888/286–7993* ⊕ *www.meridianclub.com* ☞ *12 beachfront rooms, 1 cottage* ⊘ *Closed Aug.–Oct.* ⦿⦿*All meals.*

FORT GEORGE CAY

15 to 20 minutes by boat from Leeward Marina.

An uninhabited cay and a protected national park, Fort George Cay was once a fortified island that protected the surrounding waters from pirates. Some of the 18th-century cannons that were put in place on the island are now underwater and can be viewed by snorkelers. The beach itself is stunning, a photographer's delight: the curved shoreline creates swirls of different shades of turquoise in the water; at low tide sandbars appear, and the blue-and-green water looks even brighter. This is a great spot to search for sand dollars, so bring a cookie tin to carry them back home in. You can collect only white sand dollars; gray or dark ones are alive and illegal to take. Most of the excursion companies make stops here on their full-day trips, so ask if the island is on an itinerary that you may plan to take.

GETTING HERE

The only way to reach Fort George Cay is by organized excursion or private boat.

DELLIS CAY

20 minutes by boat from Leeward Marina.

This stunning small island, the second-to-last cay in the string of small islands between Providenciales and North Caicos, has a gorgeous sandy beach and decent snorkeling; it's also a good place to search for sand dollars. It's uninhabited but looks ominous with its partially built Mandarin Oriental resort, which was abandoned when the economy tanked; the shells of buildings can be seen for miles. It's really not worth the stop.

GETTING HERE

The only way to reach Dellis Cay is by private boat.

PARROT CAY

20 minutes by boat from Provo.

The last in the string of small islands between Provo and North Caicos is Parrot Cay, once a hideout for pirate Calico Jack Rackham and his lady cohorts Mary Read and Anne Bonny. The 1,000-acre cay, between Fort George Cay and North Caicos, is now the site of an ultra-exclusive hideaway resort. Originally called Pirate Cay (because of the Spanish galleon treasures believed to be buried somewhere on the island), the name was changed to Parrot Cay when the resort was built, to rid itself of the somewhat negative connotations.

Non-hotel guests may dine at the resort. Reservations are mandatory and may not be available during the busy periods, but if you go, it will be a memorable experience. While there, you may want to join one of their classes, enjoy one of the many amazing treatments at their world-class spa, or take a dip in the infinity pool.

GETTING HERE

There are three options for reaching Parrot Cay: charter a private boat, join the resort's service ferry operated from their private dock on Providenciales, or take the public ferry ($25 each way) to North Caicos and then catch the complimentary staff shuttle between North and Parrot Cay. A $100 day pass (which includes the boat transfer over) is necessary for all day guests, in addition to any services you might use. The availability of day passes depends on the resort's occupancy and cannot be confirmed more than a day in advance.

WHERE TO STAY

★ Fodor'sChoice ⊠ **Parrot Cay Resort.** *Resort.* This private para-
$$$$ dise, on its own island, pairs tranquillity with the best service in Turks and Caicos. **Pros:** impeccable service; gorgeous, secluded beach; spa is considered one of the best in the world. **Cons:** only two restaurants on the entire island; excursions are expensive. ⑤ *Rooms from: $500 ÷ northeastern tip of Parrot Cay* ☎ *649/946–7788, 877/754–0726* ⊕ *www.comohotels.com/parrotcay* ↪ *113 rooms* ⑩ *Breakfast.*

SPAS

Como Shambhala at Parrot Cay. Asian holistic treatments, yoga with the world's leading teachers in a stunning pavilion, and a signature health-conscious cuisine are all part of the program here. The infinity pool, Pilates studio, steam room, sauna, and outdoor Jacuzzi make you feel complete. If you're staying on Provo, you can call for reservations, but you have to pay for the boat ride to Parrot Cay. Some consider this one of the finest spas in the world. In fact, visiting masters from "off island" are featured throughout the year. ⊠ *Parrot Cay Resort, Parrot Cay* ☎ *649/946–7788* ⊕ *www.comoshambhala.com.*

NORTH CAICOS

Thanks to abundant rainfall, this 41-square-mile (106-square-km) island is the lushest in the Turks and Caicos chain. With an estimated population of only 1,500, the expansive island allows you to get away from it all. Bird lovers can see a large flock of resident flamingos here, anglers can find shallow creeks full of bonefish, and history buffs can visit the ruins of a loyalist plantation. Although there's little traffic, almost all the roads are paved, so bicycling can be an excellent way to sightsee (⇨ *see Big Blue, in South Caicos Sports and the Outdoors, to find out more about the North Caicos Biking EcoTour*). Even though it's a quiet place, you can find several small eateries around the island offering local specialties, often served with homegrown okra or corn. The beaches are au naturel, littered with seaweed and pine needles and whatever else the winds and tides bring—perfect for the beachcomber. Nevertheless, some of these secluded strands are breathtaking.

North Caicos definitely moves at a much slower pace, especially in comparison with shiny Provo. Accommodations are clean but fairly basic, and locals are consistently friendly.

GETTING HERE

You can reach North Caicos from Provo on the ferry from Walkin Marina in Leeward. There are several daily trips, with the earliest leaving at 6:30 am (8:30 on Sunday) and the last returning at 5 pm (4:30 on Sunday); the trip takes only 30 minutes. Once you get there, you can arrange for a driver for the day (an expensive option) or rent a car. Remember that a causeway connects North to Middle Caicos (take it slow—it's filled with potholes), making it a great day trip from Provo.

EXPLORING

Cottage Pond. A short distance from the North Caicos ferry terminal en route to where the flamingos rest is Cottage Pond. Watch on the right side of the road, as the sign can be hidden in the foliage. The roadway in is a bit overgrown as well, so leave your car close to the highway and walk the quarter mile along the track. At the end you'll find this lovely, quiet freshwater pond where slaves would come to wash clothes. Today there's always an assortment of ducks swimming, with ferns as their backdrop. ✥ *just east of the ferry terminal.*

Flamingo Pond. This is a regular nesting place for about 2,000 of these spectacular pink birds. ■ TIP ➜ **Bring binoculars to get a better look.** ✉ *Whitby Hwy* ✥ *south of Whitby, east of Kew.*

Kew. This settlement includes a small school and church as well as tropical fruit trees that produce limes, papayas, and the more exotic custard apples. Nearby are the well-preserved ruins—old cauldrons, main house structure, and other outbuildings—of ⇨ *Wades Green*. Kew's heartbeat is still present, and visiting will give you a better understanding of the daily life of the islanders before development; it's wonderful to see the more traditional lifestyle coexisting with the present day. ■TIP→ **Contact the National Trust to make arrangements to view the property.** ☎ *649/941–5710 National Trust.*

Three Mary Cays. Three small rocks within swimming distance of Whitby Beach give you some of the best secluded snorkeling in all of the Turks and Caicos. You'll often find ospreys nesting there, too. ■TIP→ **This is a wildlife protection area, so don't feed the fish or touch any of the corals.** ✉ *Off Whitby Beach.*

FAMILY **Wades Green.** You can wander down the shaded laneway, bordered with walls made from rocks once found in the fields, at this cotton plantation established by loyalist Wade Stubbs in 1789. The walls of the great house still stand, albeit with foliage now growing on the inside, and giant iron cauldrons, once used to prepare meals for the slaves, rest in the yard. There are also partial remains of the kitchen, the overseer's house, slave quarters, and several storage buildings. A lookout tower provides views for miles. ■TIP→ **Contact the National Trust to arrange a visit.** ✉ *Kew* ☎ *649/941–5710 National Trust* ➔ *$10* ☉ *Daily, by appointment only.*

WHERE TO EAT

Visiting North Caicos is all about exploring the more laid-back style of the Turks and Caicos Islands. Expect just that when dining too. You'll find many little restaurants roadside; all of them are worth the experience, serving up local fare in a variety of ways. Chefs are often your hosts or hostesses, so be patient, as every meal is part of the adventure.

It's important to note that restaurants do not stay open late and that if the day is slow, they might just close up early. And be forewarned: on Sunday many locals spend much of the day at church, and many of the little restaurants will be closed.

$ ⨉ **Barracuda Beach Bar.** *Burger.* Though it's just a shack on the beach with a view, this is the epitome of what a Caribbean beach bar should be. Your feet are in the sand, and your table is an old wooden cable spool. And Susie, the owner, can definitely cook. Although the food is casual—hamburgers and conch—the views are outstanding and the company is even better. Hang out with the owners at sunset for stories of the way North Caicos used to be. You'll be in great company. ⑤ *Average main: $12* ⊠ *Pelican Beach Hotel* ☎ 649/946–7112 ⊕ *barracudabeachbar.blogspot.com.*

$ ✕**Green Island Café.** *Caribbean.* Located at the Sandy Point Marina, this café offers something for everyone, including cracked conch (beaten, breaded, and then deep fried) and fresh snapper, as well as burgers and hot dogs. It's a great little place to grab a bite to eat before or after catching the ferry over to North Caicos, with seating at picnic tables under the trees or within a simple cabana. ⑤ *Average main: $12* ⊠ *Sandy Point Marina, Sandy Point Rd.* ☎ 649/344–8009 ▭ *No credit cards* ⊙ *No dinner.*

$$ ✕**Last Chance Bar and Grill.** *American.* A handmade wooden sign leads you to one of the best burgers on the island. Introduce yourself to Howard Gibbs, who bought this original 1930s home and lovingly restored it as a casual restaurant and bar; locals make this a regular stop. Light bites at lunch, including hamburgers (did we say they were the best?) and fish fillets, are the simple offerings to eat while you explore North and Middle Caicos. At night the choices include conch, fish, and shrimp with lemon butter and white wine sauce. Desserts are baked from scratch. Walk-ins for lunch are accepted, but reservations are needed for dinner. Howard has built on a dinner deck overlooking the flats; add a beer in the hammock for the perfect stop amid a day of touring. ⑤ *Average main: $14* ⊠ *Bottle Creek* ☎ 649/232–4141 ⚓ *Reservations essential* ▭ *No credit cards.*

$$ ✕**Silver Palm Restaurant.** *Eclectic.* Located just behind the Ocean Beach Resort in the settlement of Whitby, the Silver Palm serves great food in a setting more refined than any other in North Caicos. If you're day-tripping from Provo, start with breakfast here, or call ahead to order a picnic lunch to take with you as you explore. If you're staying on the island, dinner is highly recommended, but you must stop by or call to make a reservation so they know you're coming—there are no drop-ins and there's definitely no late-night dining. The menu is varied, with plenty to please all tastes: grilled fish with lime, grilled chicken, and freshly baked bread. During lobster season, try the half lobster tail or layered lobster sandwich at lunch. And positively save room for one of the freshly prepared desserts; they are amazing. You can also ask Karen, the

owner and hostess, where you might find some great mid-day ice cream; her other half's homemade ice cream parlor is just along the highway at the Silver Palm Bistro. $ *Average main: $17* ✉ *Whitby* ☎ 649/946–7113, 649/244–4186 ⊕ *www.northcaicos.com* ⚓ *Reservations essential* ☉ *Closed mid-June–mid-Nov.*

WHERE TO STAY

$$ ☷ **Hollywood Beach Suites.** *Rental.* With 7 miles (11 km) of secluded beach and few others to share it with, this property can only be described as simple and relaxing. **Pros:** secluded and tranquil; upscale furnishings; daily light housekeeping. **Cons:** might feel a little too quiet and secluded. $ *Rooms from: $300* ✉ *Hollywood Beach Dr., Whitby* ☎ 649/231–1020, 800/551–2256 ⊕ *www.hollywoodbeachsuites.com* ⌦ 4 *suites* ⍩ *No meals.*

$ ☷ **Pelican Beach Hotel.** *Hotel.* North Caicos islanders Susan and Clifford Gardiner built this small, palmetto-fringed hotel in the 1980s on the quietest and almost deserted beach in Whitby. **Pros:** the beach can be just outside your room. **Cons:** property is tired; location may be too remote and sleepy for some people; beach is a bit messy with ocean debris. $ *Rooms from: $125* ✉ *Whitby* ☎ 649/946–7112 ⊕ *www.pelicanbeach.tc* ⌦ 14 *rooms, 2 suites* ☉ *Closed Aug. 15–Sept. 15* ⍩ *Some meals.*

BEACHES

The beaches of North Caicos are superb for shallow snorkeling and sunset strolls, and the waters offshore have excellent scuba diving.

Horse Stable Beach. Horse Stable Beach is the main beach for annual events and beach parties for the resident population of North Caicos. Get-togethers spring up occasionally, making you quite lucky if you happen to be around for one; visitors are always welcome. Stop by if you're a beachcomber, as you'll find shells and sun-bleached coral as well as many other items washed in from the sea off of passing ships. Of course the sand is soft and the stroll a delight. **Amenities:** none. **Best for:** solitude; walking.

Whitby Beach. Whitby Beach usually has a gentle tide, and its thin strip of sand is bordered by palmetto palms and taller trees, which provide a bit of shade. As the beach is in its natural state, you may enjoy a bit of beachcombing as you stroll; you'll find small shells, sun-bleached coral, and other ocean castoffs. There are also some coral heads just offshore for those who wish to don a mask and fins. You can break up your visit with a nice lunch at Silver Palm Restaurant, which is right behind Ocean Beach Condominiums. **Amenities:** food and drink. **Best for:** solitude; snorkeling; walking. ⊠ *Whitby*.

SPORTS AND THE OUTDOORS

BIKING

★ Fodor'sChoice **Big Blue Unlimited.** Join the kayak eco-adventure that takes you through protected Bottle Creek and East Bay Cay National Park on North Caicos. Or, if you want to go at your own pace, try a self-guided kayak tour, as their rentals are available on North Caicos. On a land-based tour, visit the Flamingo Pond Nature Reserve, explore Conch Bar Caves, and visit a local artisan workshop. You can also bike North Caicos; the 15-mile (24-km) group excursion takes you through Kew town, past the ruins of Wades Green, and to a 250-foot-deep blue hole; the trip ends with lunch and a chance to take a cooling dip. There are also trips to South Caicos to see the Bermudian-style architecture, flamingos, expansive salt flats, and the older part of town. Divers can book private charters, weather permitting. ⊠*Pinta La., Leeward, Providenciales* ☎ *649/946–5034, 649/231–6455* ⊕ *bigblueunlimited.com.*

MIDDLE CAICOS

At 48 square miles (124 square km) and with fewer than 300 residents, this is the largest yet least developed of the inhabited Caicos islands. The landscape is unique in that a limestone ridge runs to about 125 feet above sea level, creating dramatic cliffs on the northwest shoreline; a quick glance down the waterfront from Mudjin Harbour is reminiscent of the south coast of England. There is also the largest cave system in the Lucayan Archipelago on Middle Caicos. Rambling trails along the coast are an easy hike; the Crossing Place Trail, maintained by the TCI National Trust, follows the path used by early settlers to connect the islands. Inland are quiet settlements with friendly residents.

North Caicos and Middle Caicos are linked by a causeway, which is slated for a much-needed upgrade, so it's possible to take a ferry from Provo to North Caicos, rent a car, and explore both North Caicos and Middle Caicos in a single day if you get an early start.

NORTH CAICOS IN A DAY

From Provo a wonderful ferry service runs out of Walkin Marina in Leeward; it's comfortable, efficient, and timely, taking only about 30 minutes each way. Not only does it get you to North, but it's also a great way to have a quick overview of all the cays that lie between Provo and North, with views of some of the homes of the rich and famous along the shores of secluded Parrot Cay.

Visitors to North can hire a driver ($300 per day for group of four), go with a tour company such as Big Blue Unlimited, or prearrange a car rental. There are several rental companies that can arrange to have a car waiting for you at the Sandy Point ferry dock. If you miss the last ferry back, a private charter is the only alternative, at a high cost. Avoid Sunday, as many places are closed.

An afternoon drive around the island is well worth it for those who wish to know the real side to this country. Near the settlement of Kew you'll find the ruins of Wade's Green Plantation (⇨ See Exploring North Caicos, above). If you want to see the plantation, you need to make arrangements with the TCI National Trust in advance; otherwise, the entrance will be chained. These are the country's best ruins, so it's worth making the call.

A visit is not complete without a quick stop at Flamingo Pond, which is home to the country's largest resident flock.

Close by is Cottage Pond, a historical site connected to plantation days but also a nice refuge for those wishing to visit a watery habitat quite different from what you find throughout the islands; a variety of birds make this their home.

You can also stop and visit several beaches, snorkel at Three Mary Cays, and watch for the Caicos crows cawing in the trees overhead. Note that many of the feathery-looking coniferous trees growing around North are the Caicos pine (otherwise known as the Caribbean pine), the country's national tree. And do stop at one of the little roadside bars or eateries to grab a cold drink. Don't be shy! If you're lucky, you will arrive when a couple of the local gentlemen are just beginning their heated rally of dominoes.

GETTING HERE

The only way to reach Middle Caicos is by car (over the causeway that connects it to North Caicos), by private boat, or by organized tour.

EXPLORING

FAMILY **Conch Bar Caves.** These limestone caves have good examples of stalactites and stalagmites, as well as small—and slightly eerie—underground bodies of water. Archaeologists have discovered Lucayan artifacts in the caves and the surrounding area; these natives to the island would have used the caves to weather storm season. Currently, the caves are inhabited by five species of bats—some of which are endangered and bring scientists here annually to study them—but they don't bother visitors. Visits can be arranged through TCIs National Trust. Guides provide flashlights and a sense of humor. It's best to wear sturdy shoes, as the ground is rocky and damp in places. If you don't have much time, Indian Cave is a smaller version that's worth exploring. Watch for the sign on your right after leaving the causeway. It's only a few steps off the road. ⊠ *Conch Bar*.

WHERE TO EAT

$$ ✕**Daniel's Café.** *Caribbean.* Chef Daniel and his son Devon opened this café to serve the island's 250 full-time residents, overnight visitors, and day-trippers from North Caicos and Provo. The outdoor deck has beautiful views of the ocean. Food is simple and fresh: conch, fish, peas and rice, and salads with homemade baked bread. The restaurant is also home to the nonprofit Middle Co-Op Shop, which promotes all things made locally. ■TIP➔ **Reservations are required for the three-course dinners that are offered twice weekly; they fill up quickly and the cook needs to know how many to prepare for ahead of time.** ⑤ *Average main: $17* ⊠ *Oceanfront, Conch Bar* ☎ *649/946–6132* ⊘ *Closed Mon.*

★ Fodor'sChoice ✕**Mudjin Bar and Grill.** *Caribbean.* The view
$$ alone from the outside deck overlooking the dramatically stunning Mudjin Harbour makes a meal here worthwhile. The food is great, with its presentation as beautiful as the setting. Standouts for lunch are the mini–lobster clubs with pineapple-and-avocado mayo (in season), sweet potato fries, and—of course—the conch fritters with balsamic reduction and roasted garlic aioli, plus pulled pork sandwiches with caramelized island fruit. For dinner, try the chipotle southern fried chicken or the ceviche with pico

de gallo. Prices are less than you would pay in Provo, though the quality of the food is just as good as that in some of the more upscale and expensive restaurants there. ■TIP➔ **Walk-ins are fine for lunch, but reservations for dinner are essential.** ⑤ *Average main: $15* ⊠ *Blue Horizon Resort, Mudjin Harbour* ☎ *649/946–6141* ⚑ *Reservations essential* ⊘ *Closed Sun.*

WHERE TO STAY

★ **Fodor's**Choice ☒ **Blue Horizon Resort.** *Hotel.* At this property
$$ dramatic cliffs skirt one of the most beautiful beaches in the Turks and Caicos and blue tin-roofed cottages dot the hillsides, all with outstanding views of the coastline and reef beyond. **Pros:** breathtaking views of Mudjin Harbour from the rooms; lack of development makes you feel like you're away from it all. **Cons:** need a car to explore; probably too isolated for some; three-night minimum. ⑤ *Rooms from: $290* ⊠ *Mudjin Harbour* ☎ *649/946–6141* ⊕ *www. bhresort.com* ⇱ *5 cottages, 2 villas* ⦿ *No meals.*

BEACHES

Middle Caicos is blessed with two particularly stunning beaches, Mudjin Harbour and Bambarra Beach, as well as the untamed stretches of Haulover Beach and Wild Cow Run, both on the very far northeast part of the island.

Bambarra Beach. As with all Middle Caicos beaches, Bambarra seems to stretch on forever, shaded by casuarina trees and littered with refuse from the sea. Visiting Bambarra Beach means no amenities, but enjoying a picnic lunch here provides a lifetime memory. Water is shallow, with coral heads nearby so that snorkeling is possible. Stroll on the beach or out to a nearby cay. Watch for rays and juvenile sharks as they patrol the shoreline. Probably the only time you will see others here is when a community gathering takes place; each Valentine's Day Bambarra Beach hosts the Middle Caicos Model Sailboat Race, which features hand-carved boats painted in bright colors as well as local music and a number of food and beverage stalls. **Amenities:** none. **Best for:** solitude; walking.

Haulover Beach. Don't be put off by the overgrown roundabout, beacuse if you carry on to the left, you'll find yourself at a wide swooping bay. There are miles to stroll, trees for shade, and only the odd photographer to meet along the way. The water is crystal-clear and shallow, and the entire bay is a protected haven. This is where the boats would moor, bringing goods in to the nearby plantation and taking out what they wished to sell. If you cross over the rise where the unfinished home sits, you will find an unprotected coastline, a beachcomber's delight. As an aside, you will pass Haulover Plantation on the drive out. There's a wonderful little path that winds through the indigenous underbrush bordered by low rock walls that lead you to the ruins. The walk out and back takes about 30 minutes. **Amenities:** none. **Best for:** solitude; walking. ⊹ *Head toward Lorimers; take the road to your left right before the settlement's and follow that parallel to the water on your right.*

Mudjin Harbour Beach. You can hike the trails on the cliffs overlooking Mudjin Harbour and then dip down a hidden staircase to your own private cove if you're looking for total privacy. The main beach, accessible from Blue Horizon Resort, is the beginning of miles that you can stroll. The point of land that joins it to Dragon Cay at low tide is often littered with sea glass. Little tidal pools between the cay and beach also provide endless entertainment when the wave action is minimal. But as this is Mudjin Harbour, a bit of bodysurfing can be had, because a break in the reef allows larger waves to make it to shore. Kids love it, and it's relatively safe, as there is little rip on most days. Just remember that there's no lifeguard on duty. Shade can be found in the giant, cavelike overhang at the base of the path down to the water—perfect for getting out of the sun. Of course, there's always the possibility of spending a bit of time in the spectacularly placed restaurant overlooking the harbor; great food, drinks, and viewing are provided. **Amenities:** food and drink. **Best for:** swimming; walking. ✉ *Mudjin Harbour.*

Wild Cow Run. If you're feeling adventurous and want to explore an amazing strand, check out Wild Cow Run. It's at the end of the island, and you're likely to have the beach, as well as the views of the channel and Joe Grant's Cay, all to yourself. Numerous sandbars form at low tide, and beachcoming is at its best; you'll probably stumble upon the hull of a boat or two that lost the battle against Mother Nature. **Amenities:** none. **Best for:** solitude; walking. ⊹ *far northeastern end of the island.*

A DAY IN MIDDLE CAICOS

After picking up your car from the ferry dock in North Caicos, head for the causeway to Middle Caicos. As a general guideline, the trip from the ferry to Bambarra Beach can take up to 60 minutes, with only a brief stop along the way. Once you're over the causeway, it's fairly straightforward; there is only one main road the length of Middle Caicos. You'll see the blue roofs of Blue Horizon Resort on the hilltops almost immediately on your left. Either turn in for the pleasure of visiting Mudjin Harbour and an amazing restaurant or bypass the entrance to save it for later and watch for the Indian Cave sign on your left for your brief visit there. It is a lovely photographic location, with vines climbing up through sinkhole entries. Continue along the highway until you come to the sharp turn to the left into Conch Bar. If you go straight, you find yourself on the road to the Conch Bar Caves. If you forgot to make arrangements, you can try stopping in to see if there are any guides present to make a viewing. Again, this cave system is well worth the visit. Conch Bar is a small settlement with a couple of turns, but all roads eventually lead back to the main highway. Be sure to stop in at Daniel's Café and the Middle Caicos Co-Op. Just past the deck of the restaurant you'll find a much less traveled road. This is passable by car, and makes for a lovely, slow drive along the coastline. Not far after that "trail" winds its way to meet the road, there will be a wide sweep in the otherwise straight road. Keep your eyes open for the knee-high "Bambarra Beach" sign just after the bend. The beach has several tiki huts built for community gatherings, as well as very tall coastal trees that offer shade. At low tide you can walk out to a small cay for something to do. Follow the sandy laneway until you see the beach ahead. Bring bug spray and refreshments; there are no shops nearby. Back to the main hard-topped road, farther along is the wee settlement of Bambarra; if you blink, you'll miss it. Continue along and visit Lorimers; try to pick out the home on the left with fishing buoys and other paraphernalia hanging in the trees. The turn just before Lorimers takes you out to Haulover Plantation, Haulover Beach, and Wild Cow Run. It's a very, very full day if you plan to take it all in, and don't forget how long it takes to make it back to the ferry terminal!

SPORTS AND THE OUTDOORS

CAVE TOURS

Cardinal Arthur. Although exploring Middle Caicos on your own can be fun, a guided tour with Cardinal can illuminate the island's secret spots, from caves to where flamingos flock. He has lived on Middle Caicos his entire life, so his stories go back years and years, and his knowledge of the local flora and fauna satiates the appetite of budding naturalists. He is able to tell you the history of every nook and cranny of both Middle and North, as well as drop you off on hidden beaches—some accessible only by skiff. He can arrange almost anything! ☎ *649/241–0730.*

SHOPPING

Middle Caicos Co-Op Production Studio and Sales Outlet. Developed in an effort to encourage the traditional heritage and culture of the Turks and Caicos Islands, the studio has interpretive displays of island crafts on view. You can watch basket weaving and engage in a Q&A with one of the artisans. A variety of woven baskets and bags are on sale, as well as homemade dolls, paintings, and conch jewelry and key chains. ✉ *Conch Bar* ✢ *Next to Daniel's Café* ☎ *649/946–6132* ☉ *Daily 11–4.*

SOUTH CAICOS

This 8½-square-mile (21-square-km) island with a population of only 1,200 was once an important salt producer; today it's the heart of the country's fishing industry. You'll find long, white beaches; jagged bluffs; and quiet backwater bays. Life here is slow-paced and simple. Driving around the island, you'll pass through its largest settlement, Cockburn Harbour.

In contrast, you'll see construction all over the island. As your plane comes in to land, you can't miss the Caicos Beach Club Resort & Marina perched on a hill; it has changed developers several times and its doors remain shut. Seven buildings are in various stages of completion, but no progress has been made in some time.

The major draw for South Caicos is its excellent diving and snorkeling on the pristine wall, which drops dramatically from 50 to 6,000 feet just off the south and east coastline facing Grand Turk; there's an average visibility of 100 feet. It is a treat enjoyed by only a few, as there are no dive operators currently on island. Big Blue Unlimited out of Provo, however, offers diving excursions. The alternative is to explore one of the nearby cays or lie on one of the many lovely beaches as well as partake in a day or two of fishing.

GETTING HERE

There are two ways to reach South Caicos. InterCaribbean Airways offers daily flights, conveniently timed so that a day trip with time to explore the island is possible. The alternative is with TCI Ferry Service. They run a ferry between Provo and South on Friday and Sunday.

Airline Contacts **InterCaribbean Airways** ☎ 649/946–4181 ⊕ www.intercaribbean.com.

EXPLORING

Along the Caicos Bank side of the island, there are fine white-sand beaches; spiny lobster and queen conch are found here and are harvested for export by local processing plants. The bonefishing in its shallow waters is also considered some of the best in the West Indies, as is its renowned game fishing. Long stretches of more windswept beaches on the eastern shoreline have excellent snorkeling just offshore where one can see stands of elkhorn and staghorn coral. In addition, several small cays nearby offer total seclusion and wonderful beachcombing. The south coast has superb scuba diving and snorkeling along the reef and wall. The main settlement on the island is called Cockburn Harbour, which hosts the South Caicos Regatta each May. This is one of the islands easily explored by bicycle.

Boiling Hole. Abandoned *salinas* (natural salt pans) make up the center of this island—the largest, across from the downtown ballpark, receives its water directly from an underground cave system that is connected directly to the ocean through this "boiling" hole. Don't expect anything too dramatic, other than a sense of what it once was.

Cockburn Harbour. The best natural harbor in the Caicos chain hosts the Big South Regatta each May. It began as a sailing regatta where all the families with traditional Caicos sloops would come over from Middle and North to race, but sloops are being replaced with conch boats with 85 hp motors. ⊠ *Cockburn Harbour.*

WHERE TO EAT

Restaurant choices on South Caicos are limited: there are really only three that operate independently of the owners' homes. The Dolphin Pub is the only eatery that takes credit cards, operates with regular hours, and offers a wide range of menu items. Ask around to find out when (or if) local favorites will be open. A couple of other dining spots are operated directly out of their owners' homes; advance notice must be given so that the proprietor can make preparations. Be sure to bring cash!

$ ✕ **Darryl's.** *Caribbean.* This casual restaurant features a menu of the day that usually boasts conch, as Darryl sticks to traditional island cuisine, with the exception of a burger and fries. It's simple, good ol' down-home cookin', but do call ahead for reservations to make sure it's open. ⑤ *Average main: $12* ✉ *Stubbs Rd., Tucker Hill* ☎ *649/242–7119* ⚶ *Reservations essential.*

$$ ✕ **Dolphin Pub.** *Eclectic.* Located at South Caicos Ocean & Beach Resort, the pub is currently the only restaurant that operates oceanside. Here you can find a diverse menu that includes burgers, chicken, and freshly caught fish, as well as some exquisite lobster dishes (when in season), Asian-influenced options, and Caribbean flavor in the jerk sauce. At night this turns into a gathering place for visitors and locals alike; it can be quite lively. If you are around for lunch, this is your only sure choice without advance notice. ⑤ *Average main: $20* ✉ *South Caicos Ocean & Beach Resort, Tucker Hill* ☎ *649/946–3219.*

WHERE TO STAY

There's only one hotel to stay in on South Caicos, but that's changing as more of the Sailrock project is finished.

$ ▨ **South Caicos Ocean & Beach Resort.** *Hotel.* Rustic and basic—though perfectly acceptable—this two-story building has small balconies or patios and views of the never-ending turquoise water off every room. **Pros:** each room has stunning views of Caicos Bank; it has the only real restaurant on the island. **Cons:** you need cash for everything but your room; not on the beach. ⑤ *Rooms from: $125* ✉ *Tucker Hill* ☎ *649/946–3219, 877/774–5486* ⊕ *southcaicos.oceanand beachresort.com* ⇱ *24 rooms, 6 apartments* ⦿ *No meals.*

BEACHES

Belle Sound. The beaches of Belle Sound on the Caicos Bank side of South Caicos will take your breath away; lagoon-like waters are warm and shallow, perfect for lollygagging. Expect the beach to be au naturel. **Amenities:** none. **Best for:** walking.

East Caicos. To the north of South Caicos, uninhabited East Caicos has an exquisite 17-mile (27-km) beach on its north coast. The island was once a cattle range and the site of a major sisal-growing industry. Today it's accessible only by boat, most easily from Middle Caicos but also from South Caicos. Visiting is best in the summer months when the winds die down, making boat access more comfortable. ■TIP→ **From South, the man to take you there is Captain Tim Hamilton with his son, Tamal, of T&V Tours. His service is excellent, and he knows the waters like no other. Amenities:** none. **Best for:** solitude; walking; swimming.

Little Ambergris Cay. Due south of South Caicos is Little Ambergris Cay, an uninhabited cay about 14 miles (23 km) beyond the Fish Cays, with excellent bonefishing on the second-largest sandbar in the world. **Amenties:** none. **Best for:** solitude.

Long Bay. This endless stretch of beach can be susceptible to rough surf. However, on calmer days during the summer months you'll feel like you're on a deserted island with no one in sight. **Amenities:** none. **Best for:** solitude; walking.

SPORTS AND THE OUTDOORS

DIVING

The reef walls that surround South Caicos are part of the third-largest reef system in the world. The reef starts at about 50 feet and then drops dramatically to around 6,000 feet. Most sights on the walls have no names, but you can dive anywhere along them. The visibility is ideal—consistently more than 100 feet and most times beyond that.

The **Caves** on Long Cay (which you can see out your window at the South Caicos Ocean & Beach Resort) are really five caves under the water that were made for exploring. The **Maze,** suitable only for expert divers, will keep you swimming at 105 feet through tunnels before you pop out at 75 feet. The **Arch,** so named because it resembles the kind of natural bridge found on Aruba (only under the water), offers the opportunity to see both eagle rays and sharks.

A Tail of a Dive

CLOSE UP

In the 1970s, during the height of the drug-running days, planes from Colombia landed all the time on South Caicos. One plane, a Convair 29A (the size of a DC-3), ran out of gas as it approached the runway. The pilot survived, but the plane did not. The wings and body stayed intact, but the nose and tail broke off as the plane crashed into the ocean. The pieces now sit in about 50 feet of water, and they are almost completely encrusted with coral.

The dive site is in two parts: "The Plane" is the main hub with the body and wings, and the "Warhead" is the tail of the wreck a few yards away. Usually there are schools of snapper and jacks swimming through the wreck, and at night, sometimes sharks, making it a unique dive. As you land at the airport, you can see the wreck from the air. Hurricane Ike did more damage to the plane in 2008, but it still makes an interesting dive site.

The **Blue Hole** is similar to the Blue Hole in Belize, but this one is under the ocean rather than on land. It's a natural sinkhole in the middle of the ocean between Middle Caicos and South Caicos on the Caicos Bank that drops to 250 feet. From the air it looks like a dark blue circle in the middle of a turquoise sea.

Sharks, barracuda, octopus, green morays, eagle rays, and lobster are only some of the sea creatures that are common to these waters. During whale-watching season from mid-January to mid-April you can whale-watch, and you can observe them underwater if you are lucky enough to be in the right place at the right time.

Unfortunately there are no dive companies on the island. You can organize an excursion through Big Blue Unlimited on Provo; note that the Turks Island Passage is too difficult to cross because of deep waters, winds, and inconsistent weather, so no dive companies come over from the much closer Grand Turk or Salt Cay.

Big Blue Unlimited. This company offers everything you need to enjoy these pristine waters (weather permitting). Trips depart from Big Blue Unlimited's Providenciales location in the morning; the trip takes about two hours. Your excursion (about $2,600 for up to four people) includes equipment, food that's been personally prepared with you and your partners in mind, the boat trip to and from South

Caicos, and their local knowledge of the waters and what you will see en route. ■TIP→ **Big Blue also offers bicycle and kayak rentals for the more independent traveler.** ✉ *Leeward, Providenciales* ☏ *649/946–5034* ⊕ *bigblueunlimited.com.*

FISHING

Beyond the Blue. Beyond the Blue offers bonefishing charters on a specialized airboat, which can operate in less than a foot of water. The owner, Bibo, also offers paddleboard fishing, the perfect option for two people who want to spend the day together even though one of them doesn't fish. Lodging packages are available in conjunction with South Caicos Ocean & Beach Resort. ✉ *East Bay* ☏ *321/795–3136* ⊕ *www.beyondtheblue.com.*

T&V Tours. Local captain Tim Hamilton offers bonefishing and bottom-fishing charters. His service is impeccable, and his knowledge of the waters surrounding South is unmatched. Tim and his wife, Vonne, are great contacts for local information, and also provide boat excursions to nearby cays, island tours, and beach drop-offs for those looking for a day of seclusion, including on East Caicos. ✉ *Godet St., Cockburn Harbour* ☏ *649/345–6616.*

GRAND TURK

By Laura
Adzich-
Brander

GRAND TURK IS A UNIQUE TREASURE, different from all the other islands in the chain. White-walled courtyards, impressive churches, and bougainvillea-covered colonial inns date back to the early 1800s. Waves crash over the seawall and wash the small jetties that reach out into the harbor; it is not difficult to imagine the small sloops moving about, carrying their precious salt cargo out to the waiting ships bound for North America. Grand Turk is the island of contrasts, where present meets past.

Just 7 miles (11 km) long and a little more than 1 mile (2½ km) wide, Grand Turk has a resident population of approximately 2,500. It's the capital of the Turks and Caicos, with the seat of government, as well as the Crown's representative, residing here. Once a thriving U.S. Navy base, it is now a laid-back community filled with charm. Vacationers looking to simply relax will find much to like about Grand Turk, taking delight in the authentic ambience.

It has been a longtime favorite destination of divers eager to explore the 7,000-foot pristine coral wall that begins its descent only 300 yards offshore. Diving in Grand Turk means seeing Goliath groupers, spotted eagle rays, larger reef shark, and humpbacks from January through April.

On shore the tiny, quiet island has several white-sand beaches. There's also the country's national museum, a historic lighthouse, and several simple, unpretentious beachside bars.

Tourists can also see the Carnival cruise port that opened at the southern end of the island in 2006 and brings more than 700,000 visitors per year. There are a variety of high-end shops and the Caribbean's largest Margaritaville-themed bar and restaurant. Despite the dramatic changes this could have made to this peaceful spot, the dock is pretty much self-contained, about 3 miles (5 km) from the tranquillity of Cockburn Town. Surprisingly, the influx of tourists has generally had a positive effect on the island, bringing about prosperity and revitalization.

The 2008 visit by Hurricane Ike that devastated Grand Turk is now just a distant memory. Except for several boarded-up buildings dotted across the island, you'd never know it happened.

PLANNING

GETTING HERE AND AROUND

AIR TRAVEL

Unless you're arriving aboard a cruise ship, the only way to get to Grand Turk from Provo is on InterCaribbean or Caicos Express Airways. InterCaribbean also connects South Caicos to Grand Turk, and Caicos Express connects Salt Cay to Grand Turk.

Caicos Express Airways. There are several flights a day between Provo and Grand Turk, which makes it possible to leave Provo in the morning, explore the island, and return by sunset. ⊠ *Southern Shores Plaza, Leeward Hwy., Providenciales* ☎ *649/941–5730, 305/677–3116* ⊕ *caicos express.com.*

InterCaribbean Airways. There are several flights a day between Provo and Grand Turk, making it possible to leave Provo in the morning, explore the island, and return by sunset. InterCaribbean also connects South Caicos to Grand Turk. ⊠ *Providenciales International Airport, Airport Rd.* ☎ *649/946–4999, 888/957–3223* ⊕ *intercaribbean.com.*

CAR TRAVEL

You can easily walk to several beaches, many of the excursion companies, and to the best restaurants if you're staying anywhere along the waterfront in Cockburn Town. If you wish to explore beyond the town, you'll need a car. There are a couple of local car-rental agencies that offer vehicles for between $60 and $110 for the day, insurance and gas included. There is also the option of hiring a cab for a more personalized tour. You can ask at the airport for assistance if you're visiting just for the day or ask your host if you are staying overnight.

GQ Autos. Tony has several cars for rent. His rate for the day is $110 with a $200 cash deposit. They do not take credit cards. ⊠ *Back Salina* ☎ *649/241–7257.*

Island Autos. Neville offers a variety of cars (starting at $65/ day), including left-hand and right-hand vehicles. He also has golf carts. You will find him at the Cruise Port Terminal, but he will also deliver to the airport. ■ TIP→ **This company is set up to take credit cards.** ⊠ *Grand Turk Cruise Terminal* ☎ *649/232–0933.*

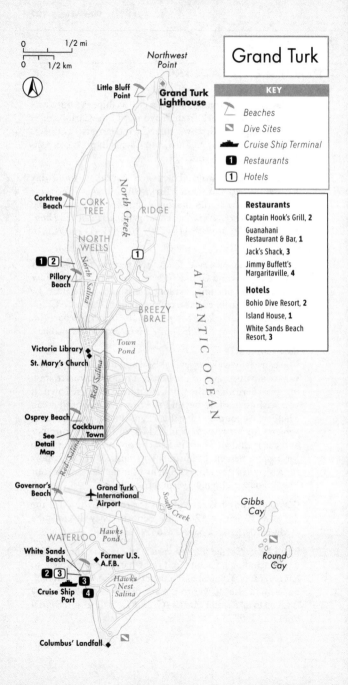

Grand Turk

KEY

⌁ *Beaches*
◹ *Dive Sites*
⛴ *Cruise Ship Terminal*
1 *Restaurants*
①︎ *Hotels*

Restaurants

Captain Hook's Grill, **2**

Guanahani
Restaurant & Bar, **1**

Jack's Shack, **3**

Jimmy Buffett's
Margaritaville, **4**

Hotels

Bohio Dive Resort, **2**

Island House, **1**

White Sands Beach
Resort, **3**

0 — 1/2 mi
0 — 1/2 km

Northwest Point

Little Bluff Point

Grand Turk Lighthouse

Corktree Beach

CORKTREE

North Creek

RIDGE

NORTH WELLS

North Salina

Pillory Beach

ATLANTIC OCEAN

BREEZY BRAE

Victoria Library
St. Mary's Church

Town Pond

Red Salina

Osprey Beach

See Detail Map

Cockburn Town

Governor's Beach

Grand Turk International Airport

South Creek

WATERLOO

Hawks Pond

White Sands Beach

Former U.S. A.F.B.

Hawks Nest Salina

Cruise Ship Port

Gibbs Cay

Round Cay

Columbus' Landfall

Smith's Golf Cart and Jeep Rentals. Some say that it's more fun to get around Grand Turk by golf cart, as the island is quite small and the roads are relatively quiet—much more so than on Provo! Nathan offers carts for two to four people. He also has SUVs to rent. The office is right outside the cruise-ship terminal's gates; on days that a ship is not in, call before reaching Grand Turk so he can meet you at the airport. The day's rental is $80 to $100. ⊠ *Outside the gates, Grand Turk Cruise Terminal* ☎ 649/231–4856.

Tony's Car Rental. You can rent a car or jeep from Tony starting at $70, or a scooter at $60, to explore on your own, or you can hire him to give you a guided tour. He'll meet you at the airport and get you on your way. He also rents snorkel gear at $25 and bicycles for $25. ■TIP➔ **The company takes credit cards.** ⊠ *Airport* ☎ 649/231–1806 ⊕ *www.tonyscarrental.com.*

HOTELS

Don't come to Grand Turk expecting five-star resorts with full service and amenities. But as tourism has grown to include a more discerning crowd, lodgings have also evolved. Most of the lodgings in Cockburn Town are in buildings that date back to the early 1800s and are filled with character, as well as indoor plumbing, air conditioning, and other modern conveniences. There are also two small hotels that were built along the west shore post-1980 and some bed-and-breakfasts. In addition, there are a few private villa-style accommodations to choose from.

RESTAURANTS

The restaurants here are small and charming. They are set either in courtyards under huge trees amid flowering foliage or next to the beach with sweeping views. Most places are associated with hotels or other lodgings, and the ambience is laid-back and relaxing. As the sun sets, most restaurants turn into social venues, where people gather to simply enjoy a rum punch together. You can count on live music several nights a week, as musicians rotate among the more well-known establishments. You won't find quite the same kind of ambience anywhere on Provo anymore.

WHAT IT COSTS IN U.S. DOLLARS				
	$	$$	$$$	$$$$
Restaurants	under $12	$12–$20	$21–$30	over $30
Hotels	under $275	$275–$375	$376–$475	over $475

EXPLORING GRAND TURK

Circling the island is easy, because it's only 7 miles (11 km) long and only 1 mile (2½ km) wide. On a day trip you can have fun for a couple of hours and still have time to relax in the sun that same afternoon. Stroll down Front and Duke streets with their historic buildings; a walking tour leaflet outlines the history behind many of the buildings. You will be able to identify the deck from which the proclamation to abolish slavery was made in 1834, and learn the history behind the families that etched their mark on the island several hundred years ago. Be sure to make time for the national museum. You can also do some light shopping at the port, but if there's a cruise ship in, head to the old prison or go to the lighthouse. If not, dive the crystal-clear waters or swim with the stingrays at Gibbs Cay, or just relax on any one of several beaches. At the end of the day, enjoy a refreshment or island fare at the Sand Bar. It's the epitome of island style.

COCKBURN TOWN

The buildings in the colony's capital and seat of government reflect a 19th-century Bermudian style. Narrow streets, designed just wide enough for horse and cart, are lined with white stone walls and old street lamps. The once-vital salinas have been restored, and covered benches along the sluices offer shady spots for observing wading birds, including flamingos that frequent the shallows. Be sure to pick up a copy of the tourist board's Heritage Walk guide to uncover the who and when behind Cockburn Town's Front Street.

Her Majesty's Prison. This prison was built in the 19th century, partially to hold slaves who were recovered from shipwrecks in the Caicos Islands, such as the wreck of the *Trouvadore* in 1841. After all slaves were granted freedom in 1834, the prison housed criminals and even modern-day drug runners until it closed in the 1990s. The last hanging here was in the 1940s. Now you can see the cells, solitary-

TOP REASONS TO GO

Old Caribbean Charm. In Grand Turk you'll feel like you've stepped back in time. Bright red bougainvillea creates a stark contrast against old Bermudian walls and white picket fences. Chickens and roosters scuttle across the road, cats soak up the sun on gateposts, and layers of sun-bleached, peeling paint only add to the charm. Islanders and visitors alike take up "island time." Everyone smiles and says hello; some will even stop to converse, as they're truly interested in where you're from.

History. It's surprising how such a small island can have so varied a history. Travel to the more than 150-year-old lighthouse, visit Her Majesty's Prison where the last hanging took place in the 1940s, or check out the Turks and Caicos National Museum to learn about the island's involvement in the space race or the Molasses Reef wreck, the first shipwreck discovered in the Americas.

Dive the Wall. For more than half a century now, divers have enjoyed the wonders of diving the wall off Grand Turk. Here it drops thousands of feet as little as 300 feet offshore. The less time it takes to reach the site, the more time you have to enjoy your dive.

Gibbs Cay. A 20-minute boat ride from Front Street takes you along the shore to the uninhabited Gibbs Cay. The stingrays sense the boat coming and then swim with you the whole time you're there. It's a must-do experience.

The Cruise Port. So you think you can't mix Old Caribbean charm with a 3,000-passenger cruise ship? The beauty of Grand Turk is that despite its small size, these two happily coexist, and fickle vacationers can have it both ways: the relaxation of a slower life and, 3 miles (5 km) away, the bustle of shops and pool games. But the bustle is bustling (and available) only when there is a cruise ship at the dock.

confinement area, and exercise yard. ■TIP→ **The prison is open only when there is a cruise ship at the port.** ⊠ *Pond St., Cockburn Town.*

FAMILY **Fodor's**Choice **Turks and Caicos National Museum.** In one of the ★ island's oldest stone buildings, the national museum houses an exhibit about the Molasses Reef wreck, the earliest shipwreck discovered in the Americas; it dates back to the early 1500s. It is even thought to possibly be the *Pinta*, one of

Christopher Columbus's ships. The natural-history exhibit includes artifacts left by the Taíno (or Lucayans), the first settlers in the Turks and Caicos Islands. The museum also has a 3-D coral reef exhibit, along with a presentation on the history of diving, and a gallery dedicated to Grand Turk's involvement in the Space Race (John Glenn made landfall here after being the first American to orbit Earth). The most unusual display is a collection of "messages in a bottle" that have washed ashore from all over the world. You will also find a lovely little gift shop that offers Middle Caicos baskets and a great selection of books. ⊠ *Duke St., Cockburn Town* ☎ *649/946–2160* ⊕ *www.tcmuseum.org* 🖃 *$7* ⊙ *Open only when a cruise ship is in port.*

NORTH RIDGE

Grand Turk Lighthouse. More than 150 years ago the lighthouse was built in the United Kingdom and then transported piece by piece to the island; once erected, it helped prevent ships from wrecking on the northern reefs for more than 100 years. You can use this landmark as a starting point for a breezy cliff-top walk by following the donkey trails to the deserted eastern beach. Unfortunately, the cruise-ship world has made its mark here, and zip lines block the panoramic view and spoil the location's solitude. If you are stretched for time, you might want to take a pass. ⊠ *Lighthouse Rd., North Ridge.*

BEACHES

Visitors to Grand Turk will be spoiled when it comes to beach options: sunset strolls along miles of deserted sand, picnics in secluded coves, beachcombing for shells as well as interesting bits of flotsam and jetsam, snorkeling around shallow coral heads close to shore, and simply enjoying the beauty of the surrounding waters. Within Cockburn Town there are small cove beaches in front of Crabtree Apartments and the Osprey Beach Hotel that you will have pretty much to yourself. The best of the small beaches is next to the Sand Dollar Bar and in front of Oasis Dive Shop; it's also an excellent place for snorkeling right off the beach. There's a wonderful stretch of beach along the Atlantic side; find your way out there, and you will have miles of coastline to explore.

COCKBURN TOWN

Governor's Beach. Directly in front of the official British governor's residence, known as Waterloo, is a long stretch of beach framed by tall casuarina trees that provide plenty of natural shade. To have it all to yourself, go on a day when cruise ships are not in port. There are a couple of picnic tables where you can enjoy a picnic lunch, and there is a decent snorkeling spot just to the right of the wreck offshore. **Amenities:** none. **Best for:** swimming; walking. ⊕ *20–30 minute walk north of the Cruise Center.*

PILLORY BEACH

4

Pillory Beach. It's said that Columbus made his New World landfall just north of Cockburn Town on the protected west shore. And why not? This is the prettiest beach on Grand Turk; it also has great off-the-beach snorkeling. As you enjoy the powdery white sand you may be visited by one of the many donkeys that pass by. The Bohio Dive Resort is on Pillory Beach, so you can enjoy a wonderful lunch or a cold drink while there. **Amenities:** food and drink; parking (free); toilets. **Best for:** snorkeling; swimming; walking. ✉ *Pillory Beach.*

NORTH RIDGE

Long Beach. Otherwise known as East Side, Long Beach is more difficult to get to, but it is the perfect spot for individuals wishing to explore. Without the reef as protection, much washes ashore; search for seashells on the seashore or examine decades of flotsam and jetsam that litters the beach, including old bottles and weathered ship's planking. You will be sure to find total solitude on this side of the island. **Amenities:** none. **Best for:** solitude; walking. ✉ *North Ridge.*

GRAND TURK CRUISE TERMINAL

White Sands Beach and Boaby Rock Point. Just a half-mile walk from the cruise-ship terminal on the southern tip of the island, White Sands Beach and Boaby Rock Point offer a secluded alternative to the cruise crowds, with access to the terminal and shops (when a ship is in port). The old weathered fishing boats resting on the beach contrast with the big shiny cruise ships that loom behind them. There is off-the-beach snorkeling; as it is not as protected as along the west coast, you must be a competent swimmer here.

The miles of beach offer wonderful exploring with excellent beachcombing. **Amenities:** food and drink. **Best for:** partiers; swimming; walking. ⊠ *Between the cruise terminal and Governor's Beach, Grand Turk Cruise Terminal.*

WHERE TO EAT

Conch in every shape and form, freshly grilled snapper and grouper, as well as lobster (in season) are the favorite dishes in the many little laid-back restaurants that dot the Cockburn Town waterfront. As tourism has grown on this sleepy island, a few more upscale restaurants have surfaced, offering a hint of faraway lands to the island fare. Away from these more touristy areas, smaller and less expensive eateries serve chicken and ribs, curried goat, peas and rice, and other native island specialties. In fact, there are spots that have no name yet serve up some of the best jerk dishes you have ever had. If you have wheels, drive through Palm Grove on a Friday or Saturday night. You'll know when you've found the right spot, as cars will be parked and smoke will be rising from the half-drum barbecues.

COCKBURN TOWN

$$$ × **Birdcage Bar and Restaurant.** *Caribbean.* This restaurant is a little more upscale than most of the other dining spots on the island, with a lovely view of the ocean, and tablecloths in the evening. There's also a full bar for those looking for their own special drink. It's become the place to be on Sunday and Wednesday nights, when a sizzling menu of barbecue ribs, chicken, and lobster combines with live music. The rest of the week offers a slightly different menu without the band. Arrive early to secure waterfront tables, but note that a table around the Osprey pool is also lovely. Simple island weddings are also a possibility here. ⑤ *Average main: $24* ⊠ *Osprey Beach Hotel, Duke St., Cockburn Town* ☎ *649/946–2666* ⊕ *www.ospreybeachhotel.com/dining.*

$ × **Courtyard Café.** *Café.* Located in the annex of the Osprey Beach Hotel, this is a great spot to grab breakfast and a coffee, especially if you're about to head out with Blue Water Divers. Leave plenty of time for breakfast, even if it's a simple one, as island time is in full effect here. ■ TIP→ **Locals rave about the fact that it's one of the few places to find a good cup of coffee and proper croissant.** ⑤ *Average main: $10* ⊠ *Osprey Beach Hotel Annex, Duke St., Cockburn*

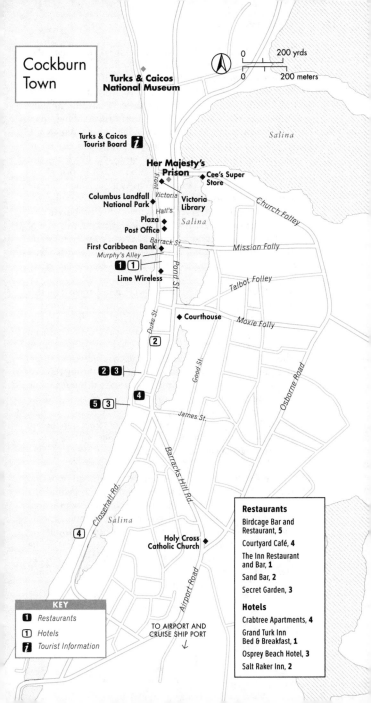

Cockburn Town

Turks & Caicos National Museum

0   200 yrds
0   200 meters

Turks & Caicos Tourist Board 🛈

Salina

Her Majesty's Prison

Cee's Super Store

Front St.

Victoria

Columbus Landfall National Park

Victoria Library

Church Folley

Hall's

Plaza

Salina

Post Office

Barrack St.

First Caribbean Bank

Mission Folley

Murphy's Alley

1 **1**

Lime Wireless

Pond St.

Talbot Folley

Courthouse

Moxie Folley

Duke St.

2

Good St.

Osborne Road

2 **3**

5 **3** **4**

James St.

Barracks Hill Rd.

4

Closehall Rd.

Salina

Holy Cross Catholic Church

Restaurants

Birdcage Bar and Restaurant, **5**

Courtyard Café, **4**

The Inn Restaurant and Bar, **1**

Sand Bar, **2**

Secret Garden, **3**

Hotels

Crabtree Apartments, **4**

Grand Turk Inn Bed & Breakfast, **1**

Osprey Beach Hotel, **3**

Salt Raker Inn, **2**

KEY

1 *Restaurants*

1 *Hotels*

🛈 *Tourist Information*

Airport Road

TO AIRPORT AND CRUISE SHIP PORT
↓

Town ☎ 649/245–0648 ⚐ *Reservations not accepted* 🚫 *No credit cards* ☻ *Mon.–Sat. 7 am–2:30 pm; Sun. 7 am–noon.*

$$$ ✕ **The Inn Restaurant and Bar.** *International.* Located at the 150-year-old Grand Turk Inn, this restaurant is filled with old-world charm; the rich wood accents have been maintained, as well as much of the architectural detailing, some of it borrowed from decommissioned ships. Meals are served on a covered patio or overlooking the ocean on an elevated terrace, and service is friendly yet efficient—not quite as laid back as might be experienced in other venues. The chef uses his expertise in Asian cuisine to create a wonderful fusion of island delicacies, incorporating lots of fresh vegetables and seafood. Freshly prepared desserts or a platter of fruits may follow, making this one of the more elegant (and expensive) evenings out on Grand Turk. ⑤ *Average main: $25* ✉ *Front St., Cockburn Town* ☎ *649/946–2827* ⊕ *grandturkinn.com* ⚐ *Reservations essential* ☻ *Closed Tues.*

$$ ✕ **Sand Bar.** *American.* Run by two Canadian sisters, this popular beachside bar is very good value and the perfect spot to enjoy island time. The menu includes fresh-caught fish, lobster, and conch, as well as typical North American fare—burgers, quesadillas, and chicken and ribs—served island-style with peas and rice. The covered wooden terrace juts out over the beach, offering shade during the day, but it's also a great place to enjoy a casual dinner while watching the sun set. The atmosphere is relaxed and the service friendly, and locals often meet here to socialize. ■TIP➔ **If you're just over for a day, be sure to get here before 2:30, as they stop service for a couple of hours midday to gear up for the evening crowd.** ⑤ *Average main: $14* ✉ *Duke St., Cockburn Town* ☎ *649/243–2666* ☻ *Closed Sat.*

$$ ✕ **Secret Garden.** *Seafood.* Tucked away amid tall tamarind and neem trees in a pretty courtyard garden behind the Salt Raker Inn, the Secret Garden serves simply prepared local dishes such as grilled grouper and snapper, conch, and lobster. Friday nights feature live music, and you'll find many of the locals enjoying the atmosphere, too. ■TIP➔ **Be sure to try their grits if you're around for breakfast.** ⑤ *Average main: $17* ✉ *Salt Raker Inn, Duke St., Cockburn Town* ☎ *649/946–2260* ☻ *Closed Mon.*

PILLORY BEACH

$$$ ✕ **Guanahani Restaurant and Bar.** *International.* Off the town's main drag, this restaurant sits on a stunning but quiet stretch of beach just north of Cockburn Town. The food goes beyond the usual Grand Turk fare and is some of the island's best. The menu changes daily, based partly on the fresh fish catch, with a wonderful barbecue on Saturday nights; you listen to live music beachside while you enjoy your choice of several mains, salads, and desserts. A special tapas menu is also available at lunch. $ *Average main: $30* ⌂ *Bohio Dive Resort & Spa, Pillory Beach* ☎ 649/946–2135 ⊕ *www.bohioresort.com.*

GRAND TURK CRUISE TERMINAL

$$ ✕ **Captain Hook's Grill.** *American.* A location next to the cruise port puts you close to the hub but far enough away to relax. And, prices are far less expensive here than at the port. The menu features pizza and burgers, as well as grilled fish, and conch fritters and strips. You'll have free Wi-Fi, beach loungers, shade, and the chance to support local owners. Service can be a bit slow, but in a place like this it's not a bad thing—it just leaves more time to admire the view. White Sands Resort is home to the island's only gaming saloon, with slot machines, poker, roulette, and blackjack tables—but don't expect it North American style. Hours can vary, so call ahead. $ *Average main: $12* ⌂ *White Sands Beach Resort, next to the cruise port, Grand Turk Cruise Terminal* ☎ 649/946–1065 ⊗ *Closed Sun.*

$ ✕ **Jack's Shack.** *American.* Walk 1,600 feet down the beach from the cruise terminal and you'll find this local beach bar. It gets busy with volleyball players, and offers chair rentals and tropical drinks. Casual food such as burgers and hot dogs are on the menu, but most go there for the island's best jerk chicken. There's a coupon on their website for a free shot of Bambarra rum. The bar opens by 9 am, the grill by 11 am, but only when a ship is in port. $ *Average main: $12* ⌂ *North of the pier, Grand Turk Cruise Terminal* ☎ 649/232–0099 ⊕ *www.jacksshack.tc* ⊗ *Closed when there's no ship in port.*

$$ ✕ **Jimmy Buffett's Margaritaville.** *American.* When you're at this branch of the party-loving restaurant chain, you can engage in cruise activities even though you're on land. One of the largest Margaritavilles in the world opens its doors when a cruise ship is parked at the dock. Tables are scattered around a large winding pool; there's even a DJ, a swim-up bar, and a FlowRider (a wave pool where you can surf on land—for a fee). You can enjoy 52 flavors of margaritas or the restaurant's own beer, Landshark, while you eat casual bar food, including wings, quesadillas, burgers, and fish dishes. The food is good, but the people-watching is great. ⑤ *Average main: $15 ⊠ Grand Turk Cruise Terminal* ☏ 649/946–1880 ⊕ *www.margaritavillecaribbean.com* ⊙ *Closed when no cruise ships are at the pier.*

WHERE TO STAY

Accommodations include original Bermudian-style inns, more modern but small beachfront hotels, and basic to well-equipped self-catering suites and apartments. Almost all hotels offer dive packages, which are an excellent value.

Hotel reviews have been shortened. For full information, visit Fodors.com.

COCKBURN TOWN

$ 🏨 **Crabtree Apartments.** *Rental.* On their own secluded stretch of beach, these three two-bedroom apartments make a quiet getaway that is far enough from the cruise-ship port to give you some peace and quiet but still within walking distance of Duke and Front streets. **Pros:** private beachfront; self-catering; the art on the walls adds a tropical touch. **Cons:** hard to find; a longer walk to restaurants than from hotels in town; five-night minimum makes it hard to use as a base for a quick trip from Provo. ⑤ *Rooms from: $220 ⊠ Close Hall Rd., Cockburn Town* ☏ 978/270–1698 ⊕ *www.grandturkvacationrental.com* ⌁ *3 2-bedroom apartments* ⑩ *No meals* ⌁ *5-night min.*

$$ 🏨 **Grand Turk Inn Bed & Breakfast.** *B&B/Inn.* Staying at this true bed-and-breakfast, one of just a few in all the Turks and Caicos, gives you a feel for the way the Caribbean used to be, without requiring you to give up comfort. **Pros:** charming 150-year-old Caribbean clapboard house; faces the beach; all guests lent a local cell phone; fantastic little on-site shop. **Cons:** no kids under 16. ⑤ *Rooms from: $300 ⊠ Front St., Cockburn Town* ☏ 649/946–2827 ⊕ *www.grandturkinn.com* ⌁ *5 rooms* ⑩ *Breakfast.*

★ **Fodor's**Choice 🏨 **Osprey Beach Hotel.** *Hotel.* Veteran hotelier **$** Jenny Smith has transformed this two-story oceanfront hotel with artistic touches: palms, frangipani, and brilliant bougainvillea frame it like a painting. **Pros:** within walking distance of everything Duke and Front streets

Of Hurricanes and Wild Weather

Since 1984, when the increase in tourism began here, the Turks and Caicos have largely escaped the wrath of hurricanes and tropical storms that have battered the nearby Bahamas regularly. However, in September 2008 the islands received a double whammy: back-to-back hurricanes—Hurricane Hanna and Hurricane Ike were just a week apart. During Hanna, a Category 1 storm, the eye passed over Provo an unusual three times; the storm then remained stationary over the island for almost four full days, dumping rain 24 hours a day. No one had prepared for Hanna, because forecasts had not shown it passing anywhere close to Provo. Unfortunately, less than a week later, Hurricane Ike passed through the island chain. Most buildings on Provo lost roof shingles and basic landscaping, but the island miraculously bounced back fairly quickly—given that it was a Category 4.

On Grand Turk, Salt Cay, and South Caicos it was a different story entirely. There was so much destruction and disarray that it took months just to restore power to the islands. Construction companies from Provo sent workers over quickly to help restore these harder-hit islands, and the cruise lines that call in to Grand Turk also sent help so that the cruise stops could resume with only a month's hesitation in their schedule. In 2011 Hurricane Irene hit Turks and Caicos as a Category 2, but this time everyone was prepared, and the storm caused no major damage.

Today it's as if these storms never happened. If you are traveling to the islands during hurricane season, it's always wise to get travel insurance: you are not really in danger visiting TCI, but if the flights are canceled or your hotel closes, you're covered. If a hurricane occurs while you're there, airlines add additional flights so that all wishing to leave can catch a flight out. If you want to ride it out, the resorts are built to withstand almost anything. Storms travel quickly, often with beautiful blue days right behind—and most likely another major hurricane won't strike for another 50 years.

have to offer, including all restaurants and excursions. **Cons:** three-night minimum; rocky beachfront; very thin walls, so privacy can be an issue; courtyard suites lack the atmosphere. ⑤ *Rooms from: $225* ⊠ *Duke St., Cockburn Town* ☎ *649/946-2666* ⊕ *www.ospreybeachhotel.com* ⇥ *11 rooms, 16 suites* ⦿ *No meals.*

$ 🏨 **Salt Raker Inn.** *B&B/Inn.* A large anchor on the sun-dappled pathway marks the entrance to this 19th-century house, which is now an unpretentious inn that was built by a shipwright and has a large, breezy balcony with commanding views over the sea, as well as wonderfully quirky little nautical features left from the original building. **Pros:** ambience and character; an easy walk to everything on Front and Duke streets. **Cons:** the lack of no-smoking rooms; older bathrooms. ⑤ *Rooms from: $115* ✉ *Duke St., Cockburn Town* ☎ *649/946–2260* ⊕ *www.hotelsaltraker. com* 🛏 *10 rooms, 3 suites* ⎮⊙⎮ *No meals.*

PILLORY BEACH

$ 🏨 **Bohio Dive Resort and Spa.** *Resort.* Divers are drawn to this basic yet comfortable hotel, whose on-site dive shop means there's no wait for some of the world's best diving. **Pros:** Guanahani is a great restaurant; on a gorgeous beach; steps away from awesome snorkeling. **Cons:** three-night minimum doesn't allow for quick getaways from Provo. ⑤ *Rooms from: $195* ✉ *Pillory Beach* ☎ *649/946–2135* ⊕ *www.bohioresort.com* 🛏 *12 rooms, 4 suites* ⎮⊙⎮ *No meals* ☞ *3-night minimum.*

NORTH RIDGE

★ Fodor'sChoice 🏨 **Island House.** *Rental.* Years of business-travel experience helped Colin Brooker create this comfortable, peaceful boutique hotel that overlooks North Creek. **Pros:** full condo units feel like a home away from home. **Cons:** not on the beach; you need a car to get around. ⑤ *Rooms from: $165* ✉ *Lighthouse Rd., North Ridge* ☎ *649/232–1439* ⊕ *www.islandhouse.tc* 🛏 *8 suites* ⎮⊙⎮ *No meals* ☞ *2-night minimum.*

$
FAMILY

GRAND TURK CRUISE TERMINAL

$ 🏨 **White Sands Beach Resort.** *Rental.* Though these condos are next to the cruise-ship port with its almost daily action, you're still on a quiet stretch of beach made just for relaxing. **Pros:** on a beautiful stretch of beach; gazebo is great for watching the sunset. **Cons:** far enough from the main hub that you need a car or taxi; busy area when a ship is in port ⑤ *Rooms from: $175* ✉ *Next to cruise teriminal, Grand Turk Cruise Terminal* ☎ *649/946–1065, 649/242–5758, 613/686–1299* ⊕ *www.whitesandstci.com* 🛏 *16 apartments* ⎮⊙⎮ *No meals.*

CLOSE UP

Grand Turk in a Day

It's easy to take a day trip from Provo to Grand Turk to see this sleepy, colorful island that's completely different from Provo. Make arrangements before going over so that you can have a golf cart, bike, or car waiting at the airport.

From the airport take a right and drive to Front Street. Walk the colorful quiet street with historical houses. Do not miss the small Turks and Caicos National Museum—even if you are not a museum person—as this one is quite fascinating. Stop at Bohio Dive Resort, north past Front Street (take your transportation), to snorkel and to enjoy Pillory Beach. This is also a good place for lunch.

If a cruise ship is in port, you can drive past the airport to the cruise center to check out the shopping and people-watch. The stores at the cruise terminal are the only real shops on island, and there's also a casino nearby. It's a complete contrast to Front Street. You can also tour Her Majesty's Prison.

Set up an excursion to Gibbs Cay and swim with the stingrays. January through April also brings whales as they migrate past; whale-watching tours are possible to fit in to a single-day visit. Be careful, though, as you'll need to be back at the airport 30 minutes before the flight back to Provo.

SPORTS AND THE OUTDOORS

ADVENTURE TOURS

Chukka Caribbean Adventures. This Jamaican-based adventure-tour operator runs most of the cruise excursions on Grand Turk, but you don't have to be on a cruise ship to take part; if you're staying at a hotel on Grand Turk or are just there for the day, you can still sign up for the activities. Most are offered only if there is a cruise ship moored at the Cruise Centre. They offer a horseback ride and swim, snorkeling tours, and a dune-buggy or ATV safari. There's also a zip line adventure at the lighthouse. You may want to carry your guidebook with you, as some of the information given along the tours is incorrect. Call ahead for availability. ⊠ *Grand Turk Cruise Terminal* ☎ *649/332–1339* ⊕ *www. ChukkaCaribbean.com.*

BIKING

If you love bicycle riding, then you'll love Grand Turk; it's both small enough and flat enough that it's possible to tour it all by bike. In fact, bicycling is the preferred mode of transportation for some locals. Most roads have hard surfaces, and the slower pace ensures that you don't miss a beat. Be sure to take water with you if you head inland, head to the lighthouse, or enjoy an east-side beach; there are few places to stop for refreshments along the way. Most hotels have bicycles available, but you can also rent them from Tony's Rentals (⇨ see *rental cars, above*) or Grand Turk Diving (⇨ see *Diving and Snorkeling, below*). It's not quite a bicycling experience, but Oasis Divers (⇨ see *Diving and Snorkeling, below*) offers Segway Tours as something completely different. You are guided throughout Cockburn Town after a brief introduction to Segway driving, complete with a helmet that includes a built-in microphone and headset.

DIVING AND SNORKELING

Diving Grand Turk is a unique experience. With the wall so close to shore, small skiffs able to hold small dive groups leave the beachfront and within minutes arrive at one of many pristine dive sites. You're sure to see the larger pelagics in the deep blue, along with everything you can expect to see diving Provo. The larger reef sharks, spotted eagle rays, giant manta rays, moray eels, and even enormous jewfish are not uncommon. Although the vertical drops take divers through tunnels and undersea cathedrals, the shallower sands can surprise you with dancing octopus and "football fields" of garden eels to play with. Even thousands of Atlantic humpback whales swim through en route to their winter breeding grounds (January through April).

Dive outfitters can all be found in the heart of Cockburn Town with the exception of Bohio, on the very far northern end of town. Note that anyone wishing to dive must present a valid certificate card before going out the first time. Two-tank dives generally cost between $90 and $130; gear rentals are extra. Night diving is usually a one-tank dive and costs around $50; there's a minimum number of divers required, so check around to see which company has scheduled dive.

Snorkeling is also an option for those who enjoy the underwater world but don't dive. There are numerous sites around the island that you can safely reach without a boat. Another alternative is to join a guided snorkel trip; Bohio and Blue Water Divers both offer them. Oasis Divers offers an Ultimate Snorkeling Adventure, where they set you up with mask, fins, and snorkel and guide you through your first fish identification ecotour for $45 per person, lasting approximately 1½ hours. If you wish, they also offer a Snuba experience. Snuba is an underwater breathing system that allows users to breathe from long hoses that attach to tanks floating on a pontoon at the surface instead of the traditional tank strapped on the back. Although no experience is required, it often leads to participants' eventually becoming scuba certified.

Gibbs Cay, just a couple of miles off Grand Turk, makes a great day trip to a small, uninhabited island. Here you can hike around the island, go for a nice beach stroll or beachcomb, and then join in the day's snorkel adventure, culminating in a swim with stingrays. Blue Water Divers, Oasis Divers, and Bohio Dive Resort offer trips here. Oasis Divers also offers a clear-bottom kayak eco-safari where participants learn a little about what's both above and below the surface and how it all works together.

Blue Water Divers. In operation on Grand Turk since 1983, Blue Water Divers is the only PADI Gold Palm five-star dive center on the island, priding themselves on their personalized service and small group diving. The owner, Mitch, may put some of your underwater adventures to music in the evenings when he plays at the Osprey Beach Hotel or Salt Raker Inn. In addition, Blue Water Divers offers Gibbs Cay snorkel and Salt Cay trips. ⊠ *Osprey Beach Hotel, The Annex, Duke St., Cockburn Town* ☎ *649/946–2432* ⊕ *www.grandturkscuba.com.*

Grand Turk Diving. This company offers full-service dives and trips to Gibbs Cay and Salt Cay. In addition, GT Diving offers unlimited shore diving when you purchase at least two days of package diving. ⊠ *Duke St., Cockburn Town* ☎ *649/946–1559* ⊕ *www.gtdiving.com.*

Oasis Divers. Oasis Divers provides excellent personalized service, with full gear handling and dive site briefing included. They also supply Nitrox for those who are specifically trained. In addition, Oasis Divers offers a wide variety of other tours, including one on Segways. ⊠ *Duke St., Cockburn Town* ☎ *649/946–1128, 800/892–3995* ⊕ *www. oasisdivers.com.*

SHOPPING

Shopping in Grand Turk is hard to come by—choices are slim. You can get the usual T-shirts and dive trinkets at all the dive shops, and there are two markets on island—one at the cruise terminal and one just north of the museum where you can pick up sea salt from Salt Cay, local hot sauces, and nice artisan coconut soaps. When a ship is in port, the shops at the pier will be open, increasing your options dramatically. Several little local stores dot the island.

COCKBURN TOWN

Shop at Grand Turk Inn. Beautiful place mats, locally produced bath salts, and sea-glass jewelry, plus a wonderful—albeit small—array of apparel and other costume jewelry items are sold at this B&B. You'll even find sheets and duvets in the back of the shop. It is well worth the browse, and you're bound to find something to take home. ⊠ *Grand Turk Inn, Front St., Cockburn Town* ☎ 649/946–2827.

GRAND TURK CRUISE TERMINAL

Caribbean Outpost. Associated with the locally owned Goldsmith shops on Providenciales, this has Grand Turk's largest selection of jewelry, including both fine jewelry and costume pieces. You will also find a variety of clothing, cigars, and more. ⊠ *Grand Turk Cruise Terminal* ☎ 649/941–5599.

The Cotton Loft Boutique. If you enjoy cruising or regularly visit a hot spot to escape the cold northern winters, this locally owned shop is perfect for you. A line of wonderful cotton apparel awaits those who dare enter—you're going to spend some money! Colors are the standard white and black to go with everything, with the addition of brighter tropical colors as accents. In addition, you will find some fun costume jewelry pieces, sarongs, and a fabulous array of sun hats. Its sister store is the L'ete Boutique in Grace Bay on Providenciales. ⊠ *Grand Turk Cruise Terminal* ☎ 649/946–1152.

Dizzy Donkeys. This is a great little shop that sells high-quality beachwear and beach accessories. They also have locally made jewelry made from sea glass, shells, and other "found" objects from the beach. This is where you go if you are looking for a less expensive something that's a little different. ⊠ *Grand Turk Cruise Terminal* ☎ 649/231–3231.

Ripsaw

"Ripsaw" is the official music of Turks and Caicos, known throughout the Bahamas as "rake n' scrape." It's reputed to have started on tiny Cat Island in the Bahamas. TCI's music is made using a guitar, skinned drums (in the Bahamas, the drums are more often made from steel shipping containers), and other "instruments" that are tools you'd find in anyone's home. A carpenter's saw played with a screwdriver is always part of the band, and you might see the occasional washboard played. Its inspiration is the music of Africa, and it's particularly popular on more isolated islands. You can still find ripsaw bands around the islands, but they are more prevalent on Grand Turk and South Caicos.

Piranha Joe's. The T-shirts and jackets here all have "Grand Turk" printed on them. ✉ *Grand Turk Cruise Terminal.*

Ron Jon Surf Shop. The shop sells bathing suits, T-shirts, bumper stickers, and beer mugs with its famous logo on them. ✉ *Grand Turk Cruise Terminal* ⊕ *www.ronjons.com.*

SPAS

Spa services are definitely new to Grand Turk. You won't find the luxurious refuges found on Provo, but there are a couple of options if you are looking for one of the more common treatments after a day of diving or touring.

OceanScapes Spa. A real spa has finally come to Grand Turk. The OceanScapes Spa is in the Annex of the Osprey Beach Hotel. Services include chair and table massages at $20 for every 15 minutes of service, body scrubs, facials, waxing, and ear candling, as well as pedicures and hair braiding. Services are limited at this location, and groups are encouraged to book online in advance so that no one leaves disappointed. ✉ *Osprey Beach Hotel, The Annex, Duke St., Cockburn Town* ☎ *649/232–6201* ⊕ *oceanscapesspa.com.*

NIGHTLIFE

Grand Turk is a quiet place where you come to relax and unwind, so most of the nightlife consists of enjoying happy hour at sunset along your favorite stretch of beach or visiting with new friends you've made that day. However, a few spots have incorporated a bit of nightlife into their schedule to keep you busy after dark.

Bohio Dive Resort. On Saturday, local musicians play a bit of rake n' scrape at the Bohio so that guests and residents alike can do a bit of dancing oceanside while enjoying their buffet barbecue. It's a little more expensive than the other music combinations, but the food is great and the venue lovely. ■TIP→ **Some might say the music is at Ike and Donkey Beach Bar; don't get confused. It is at Bohio.** ✉ *Bohio Dive Resort, Pillory Beach* ☎ *649/946–2135* ⊕ *www.bohioresort.com.*

Osprey Beach Hotel. Every Wednesday and Sunday there's lively local music to add to the ambience of the special barbecue nights. ✉ *Osprey Beach Hotel, 1 Duke St., Cockburn Town* ☎ *649/946–2666* ⊕ *ospreybeachhotel.com.*

Salt Raker Inn. On Friday local musicians play at the Salt Raker Inn. Many of the local residents gather here for this, so don't miss it if you wish to mingle. ✉ *Duke St., Cockburn Town* ☎ *649/946–2260* ⊕ *www.hotelsaltraker.com.*

Santa Maria Gaming Saloon. Located at the White Sands Resort near the cruise-ship center, this casino has been built to look like a pirate ship. You can try your luck at more than 60 slots, poker and blackjack tables, and electronic roulette. There's also an outdoor upstairs deck to enjoy the great outdoors with live bands when a ship is in port. ✉ *White Sands Resort, Grand Turk Cruise Terminal* ☎ *649/232–5074* ⊕ *www.whitesandstci.com.*

SALT CAY

By Laura
Adzich-
Brander

IN THE 19TH CENTURY THE SALINAS (natural salt pans) of Salt Cay produced much of the world's supply of salt. More than 1,000 people lived on the island then, most employed in the salt industry, at a time when salt was as valuable as gold. When the salt trade dried up, nearly everyone moved on to other islands. Today there are only about 100 inhabitants on Salt Cay. Chances are you will meet most of them by the end of your stay, whether you're here for one day or several.

As you approach Salt Cay, either by boat or by plane, you may wonder what you've gotten yourself into. The land appears dry and brown, very flat, and too small to occupy you for even a day. Don't worry. Salt Cay has a way of getting into your blood, leaving an everlasting impression. By the end of your first day, you may very well be planning your return trip.

PLANNING

PLANNING YOUR TIME

As an island of only 2½ square miles (6 square km), Salt Cay is so small that you can walk around it and soak up its charms in a couple of hours. But we don't recommend that. You'll enjoy yourself more if you take your time, ideally spending at least one night on the island. For some, there can be nothing less than a week to truly unwind and get into the rhythm of island life. Start at Porter's Island Thyme Bistro, whose owner, Porter Williams, is the know-all of Salt Cay. He will provide an orientation package, information about island activities, and, if you wish, a box lunch to take to the seashore. You might search for pirate treasure, visit some of the off-the-beaten-path spots on the beautiful north shore, or watch for whales passing by (mid-January through mid-April). If you dive, you must make an appointment with Salt Cay Divers so that you can explore nearby wrecks and the magnificence of "the wall"—the shallow waters surrounding the islands that quickly drop 6,000 feet. Crystal Seas Adventures offers a number of excursions to help you get to know the island, its history, and the waters that surround Salt Cay. You'll be sure to drive past the stately White House dating back to 1835 and the abandoned Governor's Mansion. There are the inland salt ponds, or salinas, with their artifacts left behind to illuminate the history of this tiny island. And

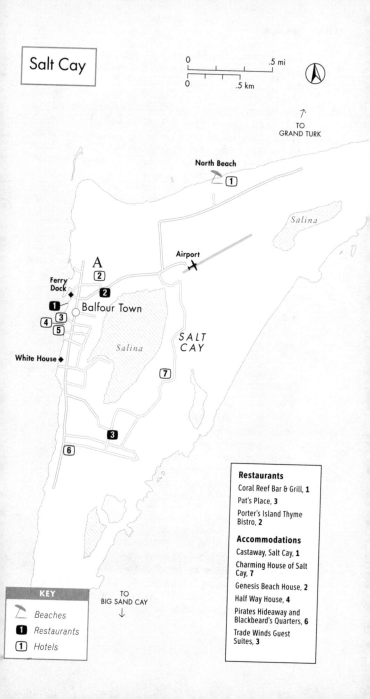

Salt Cay

| 0 | | .5 mi |
| 0 | | .5 km |

↑
TO
GRAND TURK

North Beach

Salina

Airport

A

Ferry Dock

Balfour Town

SALT CAY

Salina

White House

TO
BIG SAND CAY
↓

Restaurants
Coral Reef Bar & Grill, **1**
Pat's Place, **3**
Porter's Island Thyme Bistro, **2**

Accommodations
Castaway, Salt Cay, **1**
Charming House of Salt Cay, **7**
Genesis Beach House, **2**
Half Way House, **4**
Pirates Hideaway and Blackbeard's Quarters, **6**
Trade Winds Guest Suites, **3**

KEY
⌒ *Beaches*
1 *Restaurants*
① *Hotels*

you'll notice that many homes have embedded conch shells in their walls, there to keep the donkeys and cows out—you'll find yourself stopping frequently for these seemingly sleepy fellows who rule the roads. End your night listening to live music at the Coral Reef Bar & Grill or at bingo night at Porter's Island Thyme. If it's pizza night, head back to Porter's, because he makes great pizza. If Salt Cay lacks natural beauty, it definitely does not lack character (or is it that it has characters?). By the end of your stay, you will have made some lifelong friends.

GETTING HERE AND AROUND

Getting to Salt Cay can sometimes feel like an adventure in itself. Although Grand Turk is only a hop, skip, and jump away, it's actually easier to get to Salt Cay from Provo. There's a regularly scheduled flight on Caicos Express (⇨ *see Travel Smart*) and a twice-a-week ferry from Grand Turk (weather permitting). But if you're on Grand Turk and want to travel over, ask at the dive shops to see if someone can take you over in a private boat if the ferry is not running as scheduled. To get to Grand Turk from Salt Cay, ask Debbie at Salt Cay Divers or contact Tim Dunn with Crystal Seas Adventures. The 30- to 40-minute boat trip typically costs $300 for a private charter round-trip, but the weather can sometimes put a damper on your travel plans.

Once you reach Salt Cay, you can rent a golf cart ($75/day) or a bicycle through Candy at Pirates Hideaway. A rented cart is a fun way to get out and explore on your own. There's only one named street here, so there's no chance of getting lost—and anyone you meet will be happy to give you directions. Driving through the salt flats to North Beach is an adventure in itself, and stopping for donkeys to cross the road adds to the charm.

Contacts **Caicos Express Airways** ☎ 649/941–5730, 305/677–3116 ⊕ caicosexpressairways.com. **Salt Cay Airport** (SLX). This is just a cute little airport where you have to get there only 15 minutes ahead of flight time. You will surely see your plane coming in from Grand Turk or Provo and know that you should already be there. Note that the Airport Café is open when a flight is expected in or heading out. ☎ 649/241–7412. **Salt Cay Ferry** ☎ 649/231–6663 ⊕ www.turksandcaicoswhalewatching.com.

ESSENTIALS

HOTELS

The accommodations in Salt Cay are basic, with just enough amenities to keep you comfortable. You'll find private homes, apartments, and a couple of small guesthouse-style accommodations. Most visitors who come to Salt Cay don't mind a little simplicity, as they come here to enjoy the Caribbean of yesteryear as well as the peace and tranquillity of their natural surroundings. You won't be roughing it, though. Although most places count on sea breezes for cooling, you'll still find the occasional air conditioner, as well as satellite TV and Wi-Fi. What you do get in every one of our recommended lodgings are pleasant hosts who welcome you like family.

Hotel reviews have been shortened. For full information, visit Fodors.com.

RESTAURANTS

There are only a handful of restaurants on Salt Cay, but the food is generally excellent. Pat's Place is a home-based restaurant, where the menu changes according to what the boats bring in that day. At night Coral Reef Bar & Grill and Porter's Island Thyme Bistro turn into lively nightspots, and you're likely to see virtually everyone you meet during the day at one or the other. Reservations for dinner are essential everywhere; the cooks have to plan ahead, so if you just show up, you may not be fed.

WHAT IT COSTS IN U.S. DOLLARS			
$	$$	$$$	$$$$
Restaurants under $12	$12–$20	$21–$30	over $30
Hotels under $275	$275–$375	$376–$475	over $475

EXPLORING SALT CAY

Windmills and salinas are silent reminders of the days when the island was a leading producer of salt. Today the salt ponds attract abundant birdlife. Tour the island by motorized golf cart, by bicycle, or on foot. Be sure to stop by Island Thyme, where Haidee will immediately hand you a Salt Cay Welcome Pack with a copy of the historical walking tour to guide you on your way. Many guests choose to visit from mid-January through mid-April,

TOP REASONS TO GO

Beaches. Bar none, North Beach is the best on Salt Cay. Although getting there is not easy, the beach itself is 3 miles (5 km) of pure bliss, with bright white sand, absolutely no rocks or seaweed, the perfect hues of greens and blues, and unobstructed views of Grand Turk. It's usually deserted, and offers the island's best opportunities for off-beach snorkeling and whale-watching.

Mollusks and pirates. Have your kids collect bivalves residing in the shallow tidal pools; it's an experience they won't soon forget. Candy from Pirates Hideaway will help you search. When you're finished, head down Victoria Street in search of pirates' graves (sometimes marked only by a pile of stones).

Hanging with the locals. Since the island has a resident population hovering around 100, chances are pretty good you'll meet most of them during your visit. Don't be surprised if someone steps out to greet you on your explorations. Soon you'll be moving between Coral Reef Bar & Grill and Porter's Island Thyme Bistro as if you've lived here for years.

Whale-watching. Take an excursion for your chance to actually swim with whales in season from mid-January to mid-April. Humpbacks migrate past on their way to the Silver Banks and the Mouchoir Banks to mate and calf in warmer waters. Explore Sand Cay, which has the most neon turquoise you'll see. In summer months sharks breed here, too.

Doing absolutely nothing. The best days on Salt Cay are those when you do nothing at all. You can sleep in, read a book, take a walk, have a lazy lunch, take a nap, snorkel, bird-watch, take pictures, take another nap, feed the donkeys, go beachcombing, maybe take another nap. You may be so busy doing nothing that you'll forget to check your email.

when whales come to mate and give birth to their young in warmer waters.

What little development there is on Salt Cay is found in Balfour Town. It's home to several small hotels and a few wee shops, as well as the main dock. The Coral Reef Bar & Grill is where the locals hang out with the tourists to watch the sunset and drink a beer together.

White House. This grand stone and plaster house, which once belonged to a wealthy salt merchant, is testimony to Salt

The Versatile Islander

On an island this small almost every local is a jack-of-all-trades. Because everything has to be imported and flown in, you will find that the locals have all become very resourceful. Chances are the singer in the band you are listening to during dinner was also your dive master earlier in the day. Your tour guide might be the hotel's electrician. The cabbie you meet on arrival at the airport might also be your boat captain on an excursion later in the day, and the check-in clerk at the airport counter might sell you the jewelry she makes at one of the little shops. After a day or two, you will start recognizing people everywhere from all the different things they do.

Cay's heyday. Still owned by the descendants of the original family, it's sometimes open for tours when Tim Dunn, one of the successors, is on island. He's pleased to share the house, where you will see some of the original furnishings, books, and a medicine cabinet that dates back to around 1835. ⊠ *Victoria St., Balfour Town* ☎ *649/243–9843* ☐ *Free* ☺ *By appointment only.*

BEACHES

Big Sand Cay. Accessible by boat through the on-island tour operators, this tiny, totally uninhabited island is 7 miles (11 km) south of Salt Cay. It's also known for its long, unspoiled stretches of open sand. **Amenities:** none. **Best for:** solitude; swimming. ✛ *7 miles (11 km) south of Salt Cay.*

North Beach. This beach is the best reason to visit Salt Cay; it might be the finest beach in the Turks and Caicos. Part of the beauty lies not just in the soft, powdery sand and beautiful blue waters, but also in its isolation; it's very likely that you will have this lovely beach all to yourself. **Amenities:** none. **Best for:** solitude; snorkeling; swimming; walking. ✛ *North shore near Castaways.*

WHERE TO EAT

Although small in size, the three restaurants on Salt Cay serve food that's big in flavor, with some of the best food in the islands.

$$ ✕**Coral Reef Bar & Grill.** *Caribbean.* Located next to the dock, this small restaurant is Salt Cay's only oceanside café. You can't miss it, as it's painted bright blue and green. For breakfast, there's your basic North American fare: omelets, French toast, eggs, and cereal. The lunch and dinner menus offer grilled burgers and the fresh catch of the day. They're also proud of their island specialties, which include conch and lobster (in season), home-cut fries, and curry dishes. While dining, you're sure to get to know some of the locals and catch up on your email (the restaurant offers free Wi-Fi). On most Sundays the island turns out for chicken and baby back rib night with a side of live music. There's a full-service bar to help you loosen up and enjoy the night. ■TIP→ **This restaurant accepts credit cards.** ⑤ *Average main: $15* ⊠ *Victoria St., Balfour Town* ☎ *649/241–1009* ⌂ *Reservations essential* ⊗ *Closed Sept.*

$$ ✕**Pat's Place.** *Caribbean.* Island native Patricia Ann Simmons can give you a lesson in the medicinal qualities of her garden plants and periwinkle flowers, as well as provide excellent native cuisine for a very reasonable price in her comforting Salt Cay home. Home cooking doesn't get any closer to home than this. Try her conch fritters or chicken-and-chips for lunch or the steamed grouper or red snapper with peas and rice for dinner. Pat also has a small grocery shop selling staples. As with all places to dine in Salt Cay, you must put your food order in by 2 pm at the latest and tell them what time you want to eat for dinner. Pat cooks only when there's someone to cook for. ■TIP→ **Beer and wine are offered only with the evening meal, and it's cash only.** ⑤ *Average main: $15* ⊠ *South District* ☎ *649/946–6919* ⌂ *Reservations essential* ▭ *No credit cards.*

★ Fodor'sChoice ✕**Porter's Island Thyme Bistro.** *Eclectic.* Owner
$$$ Porter Williams and his wife, Haidee, have been traveling back and forth to Salt Cay for more than 20 years. Their love of the island resulted in the creation of Porter's more than 15 years ago. The bistro, a block from the dock and overlooking the salina, has evolved over the years; today it features sophisticated local and international cuisine, blending an Asian influence with local and international ingredients. Breakfast is amazing—eggs Benedict, Belgian waffles, and breakfast burritos. On the lunch and dinner menus you'll find a variety of seafood and meat selections. There are also activity nights—Texas Hold'em, karaoke, or Nintendo Wii bowling—and a nightly selection of tapas during happy hour, including Wednesday Wing Night, Friday night pizza, or the amazing Lobster Mania on Thurs-

The People You Must Meet on Salt Cay

CLOSE UP

With such a small population, it would be a shame to miss not only meeting the islanders, but mingling with them, too. Make a point of hanging out with Porter and his wife, Haidee, of Porter's Island Thyme. They know everything about Salt Cay and can reach anyone on the island for you. They will also provide you with a Salt Cay Welcome Pack that will guide you through your stay. Debbie of Salt Cay Divers also knows everyone and can help make arrangements for everything from getting there to food staples. Tim of Crystal Seas Adventures lives in the home his ancestors built in the mid-1800s; he's proud to show island guests through the historic White House. Last but not least, there's Candy of Pirates Hideaway. She is artistic and colorful, and no one knows the history of these islands like she does. Do not leave Salt Cay without meeting these individuals; they may be your friends for life.

5

day (in season). There's also a small shop (⇨ *see shopping section*) with gifts and tourist information. ■TIP➔ **Reservations are essential and must be made by 3 pm for dinner.** ⑤ *Average main: $26* ☎ 649/946–6977 ⊕ *www.islandthyme. tc* ⚍ *Reservations essential* ⊗ *Closed mid-May–June and Sept.–late Oct.*

WHERE TO STAY

Salt Cay has a handful of small inns and apartment-style lodgings, but the majority of people stay in house rentals.

For expanded hotel reviews, visit Fodors.com.

HOUSE AND VILLA RENTALS

Salt Cay has no full-service hotels or resorts, but there are many small homes to rent on the island, and many visitors go this route instead of staying in one of the small inns or bed-and-breakfasts. Many rentals are simple yet charming.

Two property managers on island oversee the rental of many of these vacation homes. They can also help you set up tours, take you sightseeing, and troubleshoot anything that may go wrong during your stay. Their multiple hats mean you'll also be calling them to pick you up and drive you to a restaurant.

Candy Herwin. Candy oversees three rental properties on Salt Cay. **Pirates Hideaway by the Sea** is a small boutique guesthouse set only a stone's throw from the shore, with three individual, en-suite bedrooms and full access to a shared pool set in a tropical garden (from $150/night). Next door is a modern salt-raker's cottage, referred to as **Blackbeard's Quarters**. With four bedrooms and two bathrooms, a kitchenette, dining area, screened-in relaxation area, and access to the pool, it's perfect for families or groups (from $400/night). Candy also manages **Brown House** ($650 nightly for three bedrooms), an original salt merchant's home that's been lovingly restored and furnished with pieces reminiscent of a time gone by. As it is waterfront, guests enjoy the mesmerizing ocean views and cooling tropical breezes; it also has a large kitchen that's perfect for a group traveling together. Candy can regale you with stories about the history of Salt Cay, which will add to your stay. ☎ 649/244–1407 ⊕ *Pirates Hideaway: www. saltcay.tc; Brown House: saltcaywaterfront.com.*

Debbie Manos. As well as running the long-respected Salt Cay Divers, Debbie oversees a few guest properties on island. **Trade Winds Guest Suites** (from $133/night) is just down from the dive shop, Coral Reef Bar and Grille, and the island dock. It offers five bright and spacious, air-conditioned, one-bedroom suites that each accommodate four comfortably (one queen bed with a sofa-sleeper in the common room). Kitchens allow you to self-cater, and the screened-in patios take advantage of the Trade Winds' waterfront location; bicycles come with the rental. The quaint **Charming House of Salt Cay** (from $900/week) is an original salt-raker home in the historic quarter across from Governor's House. It's been restored and updated with modern conveniences and attention to detail. With three bedrooms and two bathrooms, six people may find it the perfect vacation escape, with hours spent relaxing along the deep, roofed veranda overlooking the island and the sea. **Genesis Beach House** (from $150/night) is not exactly on the beach, but there's a full ocean view from this centrally located, two-bedroom unit. It's perfect for those coming to dive. ☎ 649/241–1009 ⊕ *www.saltcaydivers.tc.*

RECOMMENDED LODGINGS

★ Fodor'sChoice ⚑ **Castaway, Salt Cay.** *Rental.* Their slogan says
$ it all: "solitude, romantic sunsets, sugar sand beaches." **Pros:** on a spectacular beach; truly a get-away-from-it-all; perfect for relaxing. **Cons:** it's a dark, secluded road into town at night. ⑤ *Rooms from: $205* ⊠ *North Beach*

☎649/946–6977 ⊕ *www.castawayonsaltcay.com* ⇥ *4 suites*
⊘ *Closed May–Nov.* ⦿|*Multiple meal plans.*

$$$$ ⌂ **The Half Way House.** *Rental.* This beautiful, three-bedroom, two-and-a-half-bathroom British colonial villa sits directly on the water's edge; it dates back to the 1830s, but was lovingly restored in 2014. **Pros:** right on the water; new restoration; historic property with 3,000 feet of living space, inside and out. **Cons:** three-day minimum stay. ⑤*Rooms from: $650* ⊠ *Western Shore, Balfour Town* ⊕ *www.half-wayhousesaltcay.com* ⇥ *3 rooms* ⦿|*No meals.*

$ ⌂ **Villas of Salt Cay.** *Rental.* Among the most convenient places to stay in Salt Cay, these centrally located, beachfront villas are in the middle of everything, offering simple accommodation at an affordable price. **Pros:** bedrooms are set up for extra privacy; on Victoria Street within walking distance of everything; on a private stretch of beach. **Cons:** not all rooms have air conditioning; cabanas only have small kitchenettes; shared pool. ⑤*Rooms from: $175* ⊠ *Victoria St., Balfour Town* ☎649/241–1009 ⊕ *www.vil-lasofsaltcay.tc* ⇥ *1 2-bedroom villa, 1 2-bedroom cottage, 3 cabanas* ⦿|*No meals.*

SPORTS AND THE OUTDOORS

DIVING AND SNORKELING

Salt Cay diving is as laid back as the island itself, with dive sites only 5–10 minutes away. Dives start at 35 feet just offshore, with the wall dropping to 7,000 feet as part of the Columbus Passage. Divers can also explore the *Endymion*, a 140-foot wooden-hulled British sailing vessel that met its demise in 1790. You can swim over the hull and spot the ship's cannons and anchors off the southern tip of the island. Salt Cay also offers one of the best opportunities in the world to swim with whales as they migrate (mid-January through April).

Salt Cay Divers. Salt Cay Divers conducts daily dive trips and rents out all the necessary equipment; there's night diving upon request. Snorkeling equipment ($20/day) is also available for your own independent adventure, or you can arrange a guided snorkel trip. Stay above water and explore the coastline in one of their kayaks ($35/half day), or plan a private charter. In season, SC Divers run whale-watching trips, and they can even help get you to Salt Cay from Provo or Grand Turk and stock your villa with groceries. ✉ *Balfour Town* ☎ *649/241–1009* ⊕ *www. saltcaydivers.tc.*

WHALE-WATCHING

During the winter months (January through April), Salt Cay is a center for whale-watching. Approximately 2,500 humpback whales pass close to shore as they migrate through the Silver and Mouchoir Banks for mating and birthing. Today it is thought that many are staying in the waters off Salt Cay instead of moving on. Whale-watching operators have become familiar with their patterns and habits, making up-close observation almost a sure thing.

★ **Fodor's Choice Crystal Seas Adventures.** Proprietor Tim Dunn, whose family descends from the original owners of Salt Cay's historic White House, knows these waters as well as anybody. His company offers a variety of excursions: swimming with stingrays at Gibbs Cay, trips to Grand Turk and excursions to secluded cays, and whale-watching. ☎ *649/243–9843* ⊕ *www.crystalseasadventures.com.*

SHOPPING

There was a time when the only choice for visitors was to rent a boat and head to Grand Turk for basic food supplies and sundries (or have your self-catering accommodations provide provisioning for you). Now it is easier to be self-sufficient in Salt Cay. Ask anyone on the island where to find the shops we list; few streets have names, but it's easy to walk around the few blocks in Balfour Town to find them. However, if there is anything you can't live without, the best advice is to bring it with you from home or make a grocery run on Provo and carry the food with you to Salt Cay.

GENERAL STORE

Elouisa's. Located in the South District, this is a great place to pick up the essentials if you're staying on this end of the island. ✉ *South District, Balfour Town* ☎ *649/343–2158.*

Nettie's Grocery Store. The island's own little bakery produces fresh bread daily, so be sure to go early to get it hot out of the oven. Basic food supplies are also available, including rice and canned goods, as well as toiletries. ✉ *North District.*

Pat's Place. Here you'll find basic island staples—peas (which are actually beans used in the local "peas and rice"), rice, milk, sugar, cream, juices, and bottled water, along with an assortment of canned goods. ✉ *South District* ☎ *649/946–6919.*

SOUVENIRS

Beachcombers. Newest to the Salt Cay shopping scene, Beachcombers has an array of artistic creations. Proprietors Doug and Angela Gordon have taken their hobby and turned it into art. Using found objects from the beaches of Grand Turk and Salt Cay, they create one-of-a-kind lamps, mirrors, freeform sculptures, jewelry, and wall hangings. ■TIP→ **They don't keep regular hours, so you will have to ask around to find out when they'll be in, or just take a wander past.** ✉ *West of the airport, north of the main salinas.*

Porter's Island Thyme. Here you'll find beer, wine, and rum, both at the bar and over the counter to take off the premises. It's also a great place to buy arts and crafts; the ceiling planks are decorated with original Haitian oils that can be purchased. Porter also sells jewelry, Island Thyme T-shirts, decorative hanging fish, and art prints, including *Porter's Island Thyme* by famous Caribbean artist Shari Erikson. ✉ *North District* ☎ *649/946–6977* ⊕ *www.islandthyme.tc* ⊙ *Closed Sun.*

Salt Cay Divers. Salt Cay Divers conducts daily dive trips and rents out all the necessary equipment; there's night diving upon request. Snorkeling equipment ($20/day) is also available for your own independent adventure, or you can arrange a guided snorkel trip. Stay above water and explore the coastline in one of their kayaks ($35/half day), or plan a private charter. In season, SC Divers run whale-watching trips, and they can even help get you to Salt Cay from Provo or Grand Turk and stock your villa with groceries. ✉ *Balfour Town* ☎ *649/241–1009* ⊕ *www.saltcaydivers.tc.*

Salt Cay Salt Works. In its heyday, Salt Cay was definitely economically strong, one of the wealthiest islands in the Caribbean because of its salt. Now Haidee, the wife of Porter Williams of Island Thyme, lovingly prepares the native salt in colored bottles of different forms so that visitors may purchase them as a keepsake; use it in your bath or for your margaritas! You can buy them at their place, as well as in a variety of shops throughout the country. Keep your eyes open for them. ✉ *Porter's Island Thyme Bistro, Balfour Town* ☎ *649/946–6977* ⊕ *www.saltcaysaltworks.com.*

saltcay.org. The residents of Salt Cay have put together their very own visitors guide. As it is known as "the island that time forgot," note that the general information can be a little outdated. However, the Business Directory has a list of activities, services, and accommodations with links to their individual sites. With a great little map, it's a very handy tool when planning a visit to this wee island. ✉ *Balfour Town* ⊕ *saltcay.org.*

Splash Boutique. Affiliated with Salt Cay Divers, this little shop has art prints, clothes, and jewelry. Local handcrafted items include watercolors and acrylics, Haitian art, maps, locally made salsa and hot rubs, Bambarra rum, and Salt Cay beach-glass jewelry. There's also an assortment of souvenirs: shot glasses, caps, and T-shirts. If you're a birder, pick up a copy of *The Birds of Turks and Caicos* to help you identify the island's many birds. ☎ *649/241–1009* ⊕ *www.saltcaydivers.tc.*

TRAVEL SMART
TURKS & CAICOS

GETTING HERE AND AROUND

The vast majority of visitors to the Turks and Caicos Islands arrive by air on one of several major carriers, landing on Providenciales—more commonly known as Provo—but some come by private plane. Then there are others who come in by boat, either by cruise ship or by private yacht. No matter, once on land, you'll need to rent a car or take a taxi to get around. The island of Providenciales is relatively flat and has no traffic lights; most places are no farther than 20 minutes apart. On Grand Turk it's fun to get around by bicycle or scooter; the island is small and the roads are in good condition. On tiny Salt Cay, Parrot Cay, and Pine Cay, the preferred mode of transportation is a golf cart. Conveniently, a ferry service connects Provo to North Caicos and also Provo to South Caicos; the rest of the islands require a boat or plane to reach them, though you can now drive across a causeway to get from North Caicos to Middle Caicos.

▌ AIR TRAVEL

The main gateway into the Turks and Caicos Islands is Providenciales International Airport (PLS), though the JAGS McCartney International Airport (GDT) on Grand Turk and the runway on South Caicos can also handle larger jets. For private planes, Provo Air Center is a full-service FBO (fixed base operator) offering refueling, maintenance, and short-term storage, as well as on-site customs and immigration clearance, a lounge, and concierge services. Even if you are going on to other islands in the chain, you'll have to stop on Provo first, then take another flight onward.

AIRPORTS

All scheduled international flights to Turks and Caicos Islands arrive in Providenciales International Airport (PLS), so this is where you'll go through immigration and customs. Make sure you have all of your paperwork completely filled out, as immigration lines can be slow; in fact, on a busy day you will wait 30 to 40 minutes from the time you disembark to the time you pass through customs.

For those wishing a little less stress while traveling, Provo's airport offers the VIP Flyers Club. For a fee, you get speedy check-in, priority through security, and a tranquil waiting room with TV, Wi-Fi, and snacks. It's much nicer than contending with the crowds. The cost is $200 for the first family member and $75 for each additional person; children under two are free. If you wish to simply use the lounge, there is a $50 fee per person, but availability depends on the number of expedited travelers.

Airport Information JAGS Mc-Cartney International Airport, Grand Turk (*GDT*). JAGS McCartney can handle aircraft up to the size of Boeing 757 and Airbus A321 jets. It's

a full-service airport with a restaurant that's open when public flights are due in and go out. ✉ *Grand Turk* ☎ *649/946–2659.* **Pine Cay Airport** (*PIC*). This is a very small airport with access via golf cart–style ground transportation. There's no terminal—just a little pergola-shaded pad—the paved runway is 2,500 feet, and there are no airport landing or parking fees. You must clear customs on Providenciales, and landing on Pine Cay is by permission only; contact the Meridian Club. ✉ *Pine Cay* ☎ *649/941–7011 Meridian Club.*
Providenciales International Airport (*PLS*). This is a full-service airport. It offers a little restaurant open whenever there is an outgoing flight, as well as duty-free shopping and comfortable seating in the departures lounge. There are also two private FBOs (fixed base operators) on-site to provide services to those arriving by private plane or jet. You may enjoy expedited services and a private executive lounge through the VIP Flyers Club accessed through the main terminal. ✉ *Airport Rd., Airport, Providenciales* ☎ *649/946–4420.*
Salt Cay Airport (*SLX*). This is just a cute little airport where you have to get there only 15 minutes ahead of flight time. You will surely see your plane coming in from Grand Turk or Provo and know that you should already be there. Note that the Airport Café is open when a flight is expected in or heading out. ✉ *Salt Cay* ☎ *649/241–7412.*
South Caicos Airport (*XSC*). The country's first airport is very small, with minimal services. There's no air-conditioning and no food service, but water is available. ✉ *South Caicos* ☎ *649/946–4999.* **Turks &**

Caicos Islands Airport Authority. The TCIAA website has a schedule of all flights coming into and out of the islands, along with real-time delay information. ⊕ *www.tciairports. com.* **VIP Flyers Club.** The VIP Flyers Club, conveniently located within Provo's International Airport terminal, offers expedited services and an executive lounge at an additional cost to the traveler looking for a sanctuary away from the hustle of the main terminal activities. ✉ *Providenciales International Airport, Airport Rd., Airport, Providenciales* ☎ *649/946–4000, 866/587–6168* ⊕ *www.vipflyersclub.com.*

AIRPORT TRANSFERS

If you're staying at a hotel or resort on Provo, there will be a representative just outside the arrivals door to greet you; you'll then be put into a taxi for your transfer. A few hotels are allowed to offer their own personalized shuttle service, but most are required to use the regular service; Amanyara and Parrot Cay, because of their locations away from the main hub, offer such a service. Even if you have not made prior arrangements, there are plenty of taxis around to meet each flight. To the main area of Grace Bay Road, expect to pay around $33 per couple one way. You can also have a car rental waiting at the airport; almost all of the rental car companies offer this service. If someone is picking you up, they may wait for you in the nearby small parking lot that charges $1 an hour.

On South Caicos and Grand Turk you should make your transportation arrangements before arrival.

On Pine Cay someone will pick you up in a golf cart. On Salt Cay you could walk if need be.

FLIGHTS

Several major airlines fly nonstop to Providenciales from the United States, although carriers and schedules can vary seasonally. You can fly nonstop from Atlanta (Delta), Dallas (American), Charlotte (USAirways), Miami (American), New York–JFK (Delta and JetBlue), Newark–EWR (United), and Philadelphia (USAirways). Canadian cities can be accessed via WestJet and Air Canada. There's also a flight from London on British Airways via Antigua.

Several other parts of the Caribbean are connected to Turks and Caicos through InterCaribbean Airways. Flights from Nassau can be found on Bahamas Air. Once on Provo, InterCaribbean and Caicos Express Airways fly to North Caicos, South Caicos, Grand Turk, and Salt Cay.

Airline Contacts **American Airlines.** There's an office upstairs in the main terminal of Providenciales (PLS), as well as one downtown across from Town Center Mall, right beside the Shell service station. You will spot it on your right as you enter the downtown area traveling toward the airport. ⊠ *Providenciales International Airport, Airport Rd., Providenciales* ☎ *800/433–7300* ⊕ *www.aa.com.* **Bahamas Air.** There are agents at PLS. ⊠ *Providenciales International Airport, Airport Rd., Providenciales* ☎ *800/222–4262* ⊕ *bahamasair.com.* **Caicos Express Airways.** This local airline offers

regular service to Grand Turk and Salt Cay within the Turks and Caicos Islands. However, private charter services are necessary to get to North Caicos and South Caicos, as well as international destinations within the Caribbean. ⊠ *Southern Shores Plaza, Leeward Hwy., Downtown, Providenciales* ☎ *649/941–5730* ⊕ *caicosexpress.com.* **Delta.** There are agents at PLS. ⊠ *Providenciales International Airport, Airport Rd., Providenciales* ☎ *800/221–1212* ⊕ *www.delta.com.* **InterCaribbean Airways.** ☎ *649/946–4181* ⊕ *www.intercaribbean.com.* **JetBlue.** The airline has flights from New York (JFK) to Providenciales throughout the year. There are seasonal flights from Boston as well. ⊠ *Providenciales International Airport, Airport Rd., Providenciales* ☎ *800/538–2583* ⊕ *www.jetblue.com.* **United Airlines.** There are agents at PLS. ⊠ *Providenciales International Airport, Airport Rd., Providenciales* ☎ *800/864–8331* ⊕ *www.united.com.* **USAirways.** USAirways still has a presence on Provo, and agents at the Provo airport are working in tandem with American as the merger between the two airlines takes place. If you are ticketed through USAirways, you must still check in through their counter. ⊠ *Providenciales International Airport, Airport Rd., Providenciales* ☎ *800/622–1015* ⊕ *usairways.com.*

CHARTER FLIGHTS

Caicos Express can fly you from Provo to anywhere you need to go in the Turks and Caicos (or the Caribbean, for that matter). Although the airline has some scheduled flights, most of their work consists of charters. Charters can be expensive because you pay per flight, not per passenger. However, if your group is going to a smaller island, or wants to combine your trip with other Caribbean islands, it might be the best way to go.

Contacts **Caicos Express Airways.** ☎ 649/941–5730, 305/677–3116 ⊕ *caicosexpressairways.com.* **InterCaribbean Airways.** This local airline connects Providenciales with South Caicos and Grand Turk, as well as a number of destinations internationally within the Caribbean region. ✉ *Airport Rd., Airport, Providenciales* ☎ 649/946–4999 ⊕ *inter caribbean.com.*

▌ BOAT AND FERRY TRAVEL

Daily scheduled ferry service between Provo and North Caicos is offered by Caribbean Cruisin', with several departures from Walkin Marina in Leeward. There's also a service between Provo and South Caicos twice a week. In addition, you can reach Salt Cay by ferry, but only when the weather is good; don't count on it! Your best bet is booking a direct flight from Providenciales with Caicos Express to be sure to get there on a specific date. The private islands within the chain are reached by boat, either a private charter or one that's scheduled through an associated resort.

Contacts **Caribbean Cruisin'.** ✉ *Walkin Marina, Leeward, Providenciales* ☎ 649/946–5406, 649/231–4191 ⊕ *www.tciferry.com.* **Salt Cay Ferry.** ✉ *Salt Cay* ☎ 649/231–6663

⊕ *www.turksandcaicoswhalewatching.com.*

▌ CAR TRAVEL

You can most definitely get by without renting a car while staying in the Grace Bay area on Provo, but outside of that, you will want one. If this is your first trip, it's wise to plan on renting a car for at least a couple of days for some exploration; then you can decide whether you need it the rest of the week. Taxis can be expensive, with each round-trip equal in cost to a daily car rental, but if you feel uncomfortable driving on the left or if you want to go out and not worry about having too much to drink, then a taxi is the best option. A car is really the only way to go if you want to do a lot of exploring; taxis will not wait for you in isolated areas.

If you travel to North Caicos or Middle Caicos, you almost have to rent a car, because everything is so spread out. Of course there is the option of a bicycle tour, but if you're on your own, go with a car. On the other islands, you can get by just walking or taking an occasional taxi.

To rent, you need to have a valid U.S. driver's license, and you need to be 25 or older.

GASOLINE

Gasoline is much more expensive than in the United States. Expect to pay about $2 to $3 more a gallon. There are numerous gas stations around Provo, but most accept cash only.

PARKING

Parking in the Turks and Caicos is easy and free. Grace Bay has numerous public parking lots, so those not staying in the area have easy access. And all the resorts and restaurants offer free parking; even those that are gated have general public areas to park. North and Middle Caicos also have parking areas at all the restaurants and places to stay.

RENTAL CARS

Avis, Budget, Hertz, and Thrifty have offices on Provo, but you might like to support the local businesses by trying agencies such as Grace Bay Car Rentals, Rent a Buggy, Tropical Auto Rentals, and Caicos Wheels, among others.

On Provo small cars start at around $39 per day, and a small SUV averages about $69 to $85 a day. Almost all rental agencies in the Turks and Caicos will drop off a car at the airport or your hotel. You can then leave it at the airport upon its return.

There are several car-rental agencies on Grand Turk. They will meet you at the airport or the cruise-ship terminal, have you sign the paperwork while standing on the sidewalk, and have you on your way in a matter of minutes. There's also the alternative, a golf cart from Nathan's Golf Cart Rental. No matter what your choice may be, call ahead to make arrangements.

Al's Rent-a-Car and Pelican Car Rentals offer service on North Caicos.

Contacts on Providenciales Avis. There is a car drop-off and collection depot at the airport, as well as midway up the island at Bayview Motors and within Grace Bay proper across from Gracebay IGA. ⊠ *Airport, Providenciales* ☎ *649/946–4705, 649/946–8570* ⊕ *www.avis.tc.* **Bayside Car Rentals.** Located in the Grace Bay Area, Bayside rents cars, scooters, buggies, and jeeps. ⊠ *Airport, Providenciales* ☎ *649/941–9010* ⊕ *www.bayside-carstci.com.* **Budget.** This company rents cars, jeeps, and minivans. It has locations in the Town Centre Mall, at the international airport, and on Grace Bay Road in Grace Bay proper. ⊠ *Airport, Providenciales* ☎ *649/946–4079* ⊕ *www.budget.com.* **Caicos Wheels.** Car, buggy, and scooter rentals are offered from within the Grace Bay area. With all car rentals there is a free cell phone, an island map, a child seat if needed, and personal concierge service. ⊠ *Ports of Call, Grace Bay Rd., Grace Bay, Providenciales* ☎ *954/363–1119, 649/946–8302* ⊕ *www.caicoswheels.com.* **Grace Bay Car Rentals.** Their service is unbeatable, with friendly staff who greet you at the airport so that your car is ready and waiting for you the minute you get off your flight. If you don't need a car for your entire stay, there are Grace Bay and Leeward Highway offices for your convenience. Their fleet includes four-door sedans, three sizes of SUVs, minivans, eight-seat vans, and 15-passenger buses. ⊠ *Grace Bay Plaza, Grace Bay Rd., Grace Bay, Providenciales* ☎ *649/941–8500, 649/946–4404* ⊕ *www.gracebaycarrentals.com.* **KK and T's Auto Rentals Ltd.** KK and T's has inexpensive options, including compact cars as a very economical alternative to renting a scooter for those quick tours around the island. You'll find their rates some of the lowest on Provo. ⊠ *Long Bay Rd., Long Bay, Providenciales* ☏ *649/941–8377* ⊕ *www.kkntsautorentals.com.* **Paradise Scooter and Auto.** Paradise Scooter offers a "green" alternative to seeing the island through the rental of a Vespa or Paradise scooter. If you are sticking a little closer to home, you might give their hybrid electric bicycles a try; pedal away, but if you get tired, you can kick in the automatic "power at hand." If you wish to join a tour, this company offers a scooter tour that takes in much of Provo. ⊠ *Grace Bay Plaza, Grace Bay Rd., Grace Bay, Providenciales* ☏ *649/333–3333* ⊕ *www. paradisescooters.tc.* **Rent a Buggy.** Book your week's rental with Rent a Buggy and you will get your seventh day free. This agency offers jeeps, economy cars, and SUV rentals. They also offer free airport pickup. ⊠ *1081 Leeward Hwy., Leeward, Providenciales* ☏ *649/946–4158, 649/231–6161* ⊕ *www.rentabuggy.tc.* **Scooter Bob's.** Locally owned and operated, Scooter Bob's has been providing service on Provo for more than 20 years. You'll find cars, jeeps, passenger vans, and bicycles for hire both on Provo and in North Caicos. Their office is in Turtle Cove. ⊠ *Turtle Cove, Providenciales* ☏ *649/946–4684* ⊕ *www.scooterbob-stci.com.* **Thrifty Car Rental.** With three different classes of vehicle to choose from, this agency is conveniently located right in the arrivals area of the Providenciales International Airport. Included in your rental are complimentary cell phones and child seats upon request. ⊠ *Providenciales International Airport, Airport Rd., Providenciales* ☏ *649/946–4475* ⊕ *www.thriftytci.com.* **Tropical Auto**

Rentals. Tropical offers a full range of Kia autos and SUVs for rent, conveniently located on the outskirts of the Grace Bay area. It's locally owned and operated, and has provided service on Providenciales for more than 25 years. ⊠ *Tropicana Plaza, Leeward Hwy., Leeward, Providenciales* ☏ *649/946–5300* ⊕ *www.tropicalautorentaltci.com.*

Contacts on Grand Turk

Island Autos. Neville, the owner, provides excellent service. He'll deliver an auto to you with little notice wherever you may be on Grand Turk. ⊠ *Grand Turk* ☏ *649/232–0933 mobile.* **Nathan's Golf Cart Rental.** Nathan rents both SUVs and golf carts from right outside the cruise-terminal gates. He'll also deliver to the airport if you're arriving by plane. We recommend calling ahead for efficient service. ⊠ *Outside cruise-terminal gates, Grand Turk Cruise Terminal, Grand Turk* ☏ *649/231–4856 mobile.* **Tony's Car Rental.** Tony has a fleet of cars, scooters, and bicycles for hire, conveniently located outside the cruise-terminal gates. He'll also deliver to the airport if you're arriving by plane. Be sure to contact him in advance for efficient service. ⊠ *Outside cruise-terminal gates, Grand Turk* ☏ *649/231–1806* ✉ *Thriller@tciway.tc* ⊕ *www.tonyscarrental.com.*

Contacts on North Caicos

Al's Rent-A-Car. If someone refers you to Speedy, it's one and the same company; Speedy is Al's dad. Together they have been providing excellent service for independent auto exploration of both North and Middle Caicos for more than 10 years. Be sure to give him a little advance notice! ⊠ *Ferry dock, Sandy Point,*

North Caicos ☎ 649/331–1947. **Pelican Car Rentals.** Operating out of Pelican Beach Hotel, this company offers quite the range of vehicles, from $60 a day for a rougher island truck to more than $100 a day for a six-person minivan. Ask Mark, Clifford, or Susie for assistance. They will also deliver to the ferry dock. ✉ Pelican Beach Hotel, Whitby, North Caicos ☎ 649/241–8275, 649/946–7112, 649/241–2076.

ROAD CONDITIONS

Most of Leeward Highway is a smooth, four-lane divided highway complete with roundabouts. However, the paved two-lane roads through the settlements on Providenciales can be quite rough. A high-clearance vehicle is recommended if you want to head to Malcolm's Beach or if you're staying in the Turtle Tail area; those two areas have graded roads, often with many potholes to navigate around. Strangely enough, the less-traveled roads in Grand Turk and the family islands are, in general, smooth and paved.

RULES OF THE ROAD

Driving here is on the left side of the road, British-style; when pulling out into traffic, remember to look to your right. Give way to anyone entering a roundabout, as roundabouts are still a relatively new concept in the Turks and Caicos; be cautious even if you're on what appears to be the primary road. And take them slowly. The maximum speed is 40 mph (64 kph), 20 mph (30 kph) through settlements. Use extra caution at night, as drinking and driving, though illegal, does happen—some people forget they must follow the rules when they are relaxed and on vacation.

▌ TAXI TRAVEL

On Provo, taxi rates are metered and are based on two people traveling together, but each additional person is charged extra. Fares for children are only half price—but always ask first. You may also be charged for more than two bags per person. Unless you have a rental car waiting for you at the airport, you will be taken to your resort by taxi. If you're using a taxi as your primary mode of transportation and you find one you are happy with, get the driver's direct cell number. You will have to call for service later on; taxis don't hang out anywhere except the airport, especially late at night. And remember, drivers are a great source of information about the islands, so be sure to have them fill you in on what's what. It's customary to tip about 10% per ride.

Renting a car is preferable, as there are only a few taxis available on Grand Turk, North Caicos, and South Caicos. If you want to get around Salt Cay, a taxi is really not necessary. Ask your accommodation or tour operator who might be around to greet you, and know that you can cover most of the island on foot.

ESSENTIALS

▌ ACCOMMODATIONS

Accommodations in the Turks and Caicos are not inexpensive, and though there's a wide range of price options, your accommodations will most likely be your greatest expense. If you've prepared for this, you'll find this to be one of the most fabulous vacations you've ever taken. Most resort-style lodgings are made up of individually owned condos placed in the hotel's rental pool when the owners are not in residence. Alternatively, there are a few hotels without all the bells and whistles and no kitchens. There are also two all-inclusive resorts on Provo: the family-oriented Beaches and the adults-only Club Med. The outer islands have more basic accommodations, albeit with a lot more island flair. Providenciales also has an incredible array of private villas to choose from. This is an excellent option for a family, as they offer privacy, added room, and usually work out on the less expensive end. Take a look at VRBO and Home Away to see the selection (⇨ *see Apartment and House Rentals, below*).

If your accommodations don't include baby equipment or you need additional baby items, contact Happy Na and have it delivered.

Happy Na Baby Equipment Rentals. Little ones can be quite the needy little family members when it comes to travel, so it's always nice to know that some things can be left behind, as there's Happy Na on Provo. They can provide strollers, cribs, playpens, bedding, and more for the day or (at a discount) for longer. Their office is on Industrial Drive, but they deliver to any property where you might be staying. ✉ *Industrial Dr., Providenciales* ☎ *649/941–5326, 649/241–2760* ✍ *happynatci@gmail.com.*

APARTMENT AND HOUSE RENTALS

Villa and condo rentals are quite common in the Turks and Caicos; in fact, they make up the majority of accommodations. On Provo, many of the villas are ultra-luxurious getaways and have prices to match. On the smaller islands, villas are basic and comfortable and tend to be more economical alternatives. Private apartment rentals can save you money but tend to be more residential, with fewer services. On any of the islands they are easy to book, and management companies will send a representative to meet you at the airport as well as assist you as a concierge might.

Contacts **Home Away.** With more than 500 listings for the Turks and Caicos Islands, this is an excellent site for browsing available properties, including independently rented villas. ⊕ *www.homeaway.com.* **Turks and Caicos Reservations.** Based on the island, they keep an inventory of villas and resorts, and are in constant contact with general managers and property managements. They go the extra mile, acting as your concierge, helping to find you a property if you're in a travel bind, and arranging package deals. ☎ *649/941–8988, 877/774–5486* ⊕ *www.turksandcaicosreservations. tc.* **Vacation Rentals by Owner** (*VRBO*). More widely known as simply VRBO, this company has the largest array of properties published. You will find absolutely every independent property on this site, as well as listings for many hotels and resorts. It's extremely user friendly, but its huge selection can be a little overwhelming. ⊕ *www.VRBO.com.*

HOTELS

Hotels and resorts in Turks and Caicos run the gamut from small inns with basic accommodations to full-service, private-island resorts. There are a few classy boutique hotels on Provo, but no large chain hotels. Parrot Cay and the Meridian Club on Pine Cay are private-island resorts with all the pampering and privileges you'd expect with the high prices. Amanyara is in a category all its own, offering the greatest degree of seclusion and privacy, with a price tag at the top end of the scale.

█ COMMUNICATIONS

INTERNET

The majority of resorts throughout the Turks and Caicos offer free Wi-Fi service in the individual rooms. If they don't, you will have access in the public areas so you can keep up with email and the Internet.

T&C LODGING TIPS

Budget for the add-ons. You must pay 12% tax, plus an additional 10% service charge.

Avoid peak season. Rates are about 35% higher from mid-December through mid-April.

Book in advance. Resorts fill up quickly with repeat visitors, as do villas with their regular clientele.

Reservations required. You cannot enter the Turks and Caicos unless you have reserved a place to stay.

Book direct. You can sometimes get rates that are just as good (if not better) by booking directly through the resort or using the local website for Turks and Caicos Reservations. For some condos you can book directly with the owner for less and avoid the resort's service charge, but be sure to ask about resort amenities; some may not be included when you book this way.

Consider your options. If you're low maintenance, consider a self-catering apartment that will save you money on both food and resort services.

Not sure where to stay? Start by going through the local *Where-WhenHow* magazine; their current issue can be found online. But if you are looking to stay in a private villa, then it's best to go directly to VRBO and Home Away once you become acquainted with the island and what the different locations have to offer.

PHONES

The country code for the Turks and Caicos is 649. To call the Turks and Caicos from the United States, dial 1 plus the 10-digit number, which includes the 649 prefix. Be aware that this is an international call. Calls from the islands are expensive, and many hotels add steep surcharges for long distance.

CALLING WITHIN THE TURKS AND CAICOS

To make local calls, just dial the seven-digit number. Most hotels and resorts charge for local calls, usually 50¢ a minute.

CALLING OUTSIDE THE TURKS AND CAICOS

To call the United States, dial 1, then the area code, and the seven-digit number. If you get a recording saying the number is out of service, try again. This is usually not the case, and your call will go through on the second try.

MOBILE PHONES

Before leaving home, contact your service provider to find out if you have coverage in Turks and Caicos. Chances are your phone will work here. However, roaming fees can be steep, with 99¢ a minute considered reasonable.

If your own cell phone doesn't work in the TCI, or you wish to avoid the cost of such a privilege, you can rent one from a local provider, through either Lime or Digicel. Local cell-phone coverage is very good; you'll even get reception on most of the uninhabited cays. Also be aware that many toll-free numbers are not free of charge when you make the call from Turks and Caicos; you will be notified by an automated service before the call is connected, and the rate is for an international call.

If you just want to be able to make local calls, consider buying a new SIM card; you may need to have your provider unlock your phone for this use. You will also need a prepaid service plan. You'll then have a local number and can make local calls at local rates. As an alternative, you can purchase a new cell phone once you've landed and pick up prepaid minutes as you go. Ask your car-rental company or villa management if they offer free loaner cell phones. Grace Bay Car Rentals is one that does; many other companies do as well. You can add value online or at kiosks all over the island, and incoming calls are free.

Contacts **Digicel TCI**. Digicel provides service to almost half of the island's residents. They offer both prepaid and postpaid services with inexpensive models you can purchase as a visitor to the islands. ✉ *Graceway Plaza, Leeward Hwy., Providenciales* ☎ *649/331–3444* ⊕ *www.digiceltci.com.* **LIME**. LIME provides prepaid and postpaid services. You can find their office on Leeward Highway, mid-island, as well as on Front Street in Grand Turk. They have a variety of phones that you may purchase to use while visiting. ☎ *649/946–2200, 611 for broad inquiries, 800/804–2994* ⊕ *www.lime.com.*

■ CUSTOMS AND DUTIES

Customs in the Turks and Caicos is straightforward and simple. On the flight you will receive two forms. The first is your customs declaration, one per family. The second form is a Turks & Caicos Embarkation and Disembarkation Form. Both forms should be filled out completely before you disembark to avoid delays. Make sure to keep the stub from the Disembarkation Form; you'll need to show it when you leave the island. If you are 17 years of age or older, you are allowed to bring in free of import duty 1 liter of spirits or 2 liters of wine; either 200 cigarettes *or* 100 cigarillos *or* 50 cigars *or* 250 grams of smoking tobacco; and 50 grams of perfume *or* 0.25 liters of eau de toilette. If you have $10,000 or more in cash, you must declare it.

The immigration entrance lines can be long, especially when several planes arrive in quick succession.

Turks and Caicos Islands Information **TCI Tourism.** This is a wonderful source to go to for information. The office is close to Grace Bay proper; there you will find helpful staff, maps, and an assortment of brochures to browse through to assist you in your vacation plans. Be sure to check out their informative website. ☎ *649/946–4970, 800/241–0824* ⊕ *www.TurksandCaicosTourism.com.*

U.S. Information **U.S. Customs and Border Protection.** Currently there is no U.S. customs service in Providenciales, so you will go through customs once you have landed in the United States. ⊕ *www. cbp.gov.*

■ EATING OUT

Turks and Caicos has almost every kind of restaurant you might wish for, especially on Provo. From small beach shacks to gorgeous upscale dining rooms and everything in between, this destination is a gastronomical delight. There are cafés and delis, international restaurants, and some of the best chefs in the Caribbean; what you won't find is fast food or restaurant chains. Typically, the restaurants offer wide choices, so even vegetarians and picky eaters will find something appealing on most menus. If a restaurant does not have a children's menu, the chef will usually be willing to make something to suit your kids, so don't be afraid to ask. Restaurants cater primarily to American tastes (especially on American holidays). Dinner usually starts a little later than Americans are used to; most restaurants are full by 8. Most restaurants are upscale and expensive, though you will also find a few slightly less expensive, more casual options. A typical meal averages $80 to $120 per couple without a bottle of wine, much more if you add that in.

■TIP➔ Always check your bill carefully before paying. Restaurants can become so busy at times that bills can get combined with another table's.

Unless otherwise noted, restaurants listed in this guide are open daily for lunch and dinner.

TURKS AND CAICOS CUISINE

The most typical foods on these islands come from the sea. Grouper and snapper are usually the catch of the day, often grilled with jerk spices. But be sure to ask whether the fish is fresh caught or brought in. In season, spiny lobster is brought in daily—as long as the seas aren't too rough—and used in many ways, in addition to the more familiar thermidor and broiled. One favorite food in the Turks and Caicos is conch; it even has its own festival in November, with recipe and tasting competitions. Conch is made every way imaginable, including the typical cracked conch and conch fritters. Macaroni and cheese, fried plantain, and peas 'n rice are common side dishes, especially in spots that serve local food. Coleslaw here even has a Caribbean twist, often including pineapple or mango. For a typical island breakfast, order broiled fish with baked beans and grits.

PAYING

Most major credit cards (Visa, Discover, and MasterCard—Diner's Club less so) are accepted in almost all restaurants. American Express is accepted in far fewer establishments. It's smart to bring more than one type of credit card with you just in case. Call your credit-card company to see if they charge an additional foreign transaction fee; most add 2.5%, even though all transactions in the TCI are in U.S. dollars. If a place takes cash only, it's noted on the review.

RESERVATIONS AND DRESS

We mention reservations only when they are essential (there's no other way you'll ever get a table) or when they are not accepted. We mention dress only when men are required to wear a jacket or a jacket and tie, which is currently not the case anywhere in the country. Although you don't need fancy dresses or even long pants at most places, you will look out of place in a T-shirt and tennis shoes.

WINES, BEER, AND SPIRITS

You can expect to pay more than you would at home. Imported U.S. beer is particularly expensive; a case of Bud Light or Miller Light can run $65 to $75. For beer lovers, it's always fun to try something new: the brewery for Turks Head, which is a heavier-tasting beer than its American counterparts, offers tours. In addition, some other Caribbean brands are available in local stores, including Kalik and Red Stripe. Of the rums, Caicos Rum is made for the Turks and Caicos and bottled here. Turks and Caicos's Bambarra Rum is a bargain compared with other rums. Remember that although you can always buy alcohol at a bar, it's against the law to purchase it from a store on Sunday.

▌ ELECTRICITY

Electricity is fairly stable throughout the islands, and the current is suitable for all U.S. appliances (120 volts, 60 Hz).

▍ EMERGENCIES

The emergency numbers in the Turks and Caicos are 999 or 911.

▍ HEALTH

Turks and Caicos is a safe and healthy destination. The tap water may not be the best tasting, but it is safe to drink. Food-safety standards are high, and you rarely hear of upset stomachs or outbreaks of food poisoning. If you're feeling unwell, there are very good hospitals on both Provo and Grand Turk, as well as private health care clinics. Grace Bay Beach is usually clean and clear of any pests. There are no poisonous snakes in the Turks and Caicos, or any other animals that may be dangerous. Be sure not to go off the beaten path when exploring around the islands, however, as there are two trees in particular that act like poison ivy; they are difficult to identify, so it is best to stay out of the bush. In the water, be careful not to touch the coral, as a particular variety will burn your skin upon contact. You also must watch out for the lionfish; they are beautiful but very dangerous.

OVER-THE-COUNTER REMEDIES

Most of the supplies are similar to those in the United Kingdom, United States, and Canada. You can find all the major brands that you are used to readily available around Provo, though prices are higher than at home. Over-the-counter drugs can be found at pharmacies and supermarkets, and even at small convenience stores. If you plan to travel beyond Provo, however, you may wish to stock up on necessities. Supplies may be slimmer on the less-developed islands. Sunscreen is especially expensive in the Grace Bay area; it's more reasonably priced at the IGA supermarket. If you need bug spray, get something with at least 25% DEET; off-brand spray is readily available. If you forget to buy it and find yourself at dusk with no-see-ums biting, ask your servers at the restaurant; there's a good chance they'll have a bottle on hand.

Health Warnings Centers for Disease Control and Prevention (*CDC*). ☎ 800/232–4636 *international travelers' health line* ⊕ *www.cdc.gov.*

▍ HOURS OF OPERATION

Banks are typically open Monday through Thursday from 9 to 3, Fridays until 4. Post offices are open weekdays from 10 to 4. Shops are generally open from 10 to 5 or 6; you will find some shops are closed on Sunday, more during the quieter season. You cannot buy alcohol anywhere in the islands on Sunday, except at a bar or restaurant.

HOLIDAYS

Public holidays are New Year's Day, Commonwealth Day (second Monday in March), Good Friday, Easter Monday, National Heroes Day (last Monday in May), Queen's Birthday (third Monday in June), Emancipation Day (first Monday in August), National Youth Day (last Monday in September), Columbus Day (second

Monday in October), International Human Rights Day (last Monday in October), Christmas Day, and Boxing Day (December 26).

▎ SHIPPING PACKAGES

There are four private shipping services available on Provo, one in Grand Turk: FedEx, UPS, DHL, and IBC. Though expensive, this method is the only reliable way to send something to or from the islands. The service getting it to and from the islands is consistent, but direct delivery to and from homes and businesses throughout the islands may be a problem. Visitors are advised to pick up packages at the offices of FedEx and UPS, unless they're staying at a major resort.

Contacts **DHL.** DHL provides international shipping services. ⊠ *Town Centre Mall, Downtown, Providenciales* ☎ 649/946–4352 ⊕ *www.dhl. com.vc.* **FedEx.** ⊠ *Leeward Hwy., Unit 109A, Providenciales* ☎ 649/946–4682 *On Provo* ⊕ *www.fedex.com/ tc.* **International Bonded Couriers.** This company provides international shipping services. ⊠ *Courtyard Plaza, Providenciales* ☎ 649/941–4200, 649/941–4204 ⊕ *www.ibcinc. com.* **UPS.** UPS offers international services, with delivery on Providenciales and Grand Turk. ⊠ *Airport Rd., Providenciales* ☎ 800/742–5877, 649/941–4048 ⊕ *www.ups.com.*

▎ MONEY

Prices quoted in this chapter are in U.S. dollars, which is the official currency in the islands.

Major credit cards and traveler's checks are accepted at many establishments. Bring small-denomination bills to the less populated islands—but bring enough cash to hold you over; many of the smaller islands deal in cash only and have no ATMs. Some islands don't even have banks, so get some cash while on Provo if heading elsewhere.

Prices throughout this guide are given for adults. Reduced rates are almost always available for children, students, and senior citizens.

ATMS AND BANKS

On Provo there are ATMs at all bank branches (Scotiabank and First Caribbean), at the airport, at Graceway IGA Supermarket, Ports of Call shopping center, and at Graceway Gourmet IGA. There are also Scotiabank and First Caribbean branches on Grand Turk.

CREDIT CARDS

It's a good idea to inform your credit-card company before you travel. If you plan to use your credit card for cash advances, you'll need to apply for a PIN at least two weeks before your trip. Although it's usually cheaper (and safer) to use a credit card abroad for large purchases (so you can cancel payments or be reimbursed if there's a problem), note that some credit-card companies *and* the banks that issue them add substantial percentages to all foreign transactions, whether they're in a foreign currency or not.

Note that some shops require a $25 minimum to charge. A few shops may pass along their 3% to 5% surcharge if you pay by credit card; the clerk will tell you before you pay.

PACKING

Most accommodations in Provo have washers and dryers in the units, so pack light. You can wash your clothes conveniently at your whim and dry swimsuits before repacking. If your resort doesn't offer laundry facilities or a laundry service, you'll find a dry cleaner/laundry facility next to Beaches on the Lower Bight Road. There is also a dry cleaner in the complex just south of Graceway Gourmet IGA, as well as one on the extension of Leeward Highway.

If you travel with a carry-on, remember that airlines allow only 3-ounce bottles of liquids. Don't worry: it's not too expensive to buy sunscreen at the Graceway IGA supermarket. There's really not a huge bug problem in the Turks and Caicos, but sometimes after a rain or at dusk you might get a bite or two, so you will end up needing to bring or buy some repellent.

Almost all the resorts and villas have hair dryers and give you shampoo, conditioner, and a small box of laundry detergent. Check ahead to be certain. "Bring half the clothes and twice the money"—words to live by.

▌ PASSPORTS AND VISAS

U.S. citizens must have a valid passport to travel by air to the Turks and Caicos. Everyone must have an ongoing or return ticket and a confirmed hotel reservation. Make sure to keep the embarka-

tion stub that you filled out when you landed; you'll need it when you leave.

▌ RESTROOMS

There are public restrooms and a playground in between Gansevoort and Aquamarine Beach Houses, for those times when you haven't realized how far you've walked. You can also slip into any resort and ask if you may use their facilities if necessary.

▌ SAFETY

Although crime is not a major concern in the Turks and Caicos Islands, petty theft does occur here, and you're advised to leave your valuables in your hotel safe or deposit box and lock the doors of your car and your room when unattended. If you are staying in a villa, be sure to check that the sliding doors are closed and that you have not left windows wide open with only the screen as protection.

TAXES

The departure tax is included in the cost of your airline ticket, so you don't need to worry about having additional cash ready at the airport. Restaurants and hotels add a 12% government tax. Hotels also typically add 10% to 15% for service.

▌ TIME

The Turks and Caicos Islands are on Eastern Standard Time, the same as New York City and Atlanta. Unlike most Caribbean destinations, the Turks and Caicos have followed daylight saving time as the United States does. However, there is the possibility that this will change in 2016; it is currently tabled for government acceptance. Club Med has paved the way, as they do not change their clocks, making them an hour earlier than those on the rest of the island during months when daylight saving time is in effect.

TIPPING

Check your bill to see if a 10% service charge has been added. If it has, you may supplement it by 5% or even more if service was outstanding. If no service charge has been added, then tip as you would at home, about 15%. *Be aware that when a large party dines together, a hefty service fee may be added at the end.*

The current government tax is 12%, which is mandatory for all diners.

Taxi drivers also expect a tip, about 10% of your fare. Excursion and water-sports staff appreciate tips for their efforts as well; use your discretion.

VISITOR INFORMATION

The tourist offices on Grand Turk and Providenciales are open daily from 9 to 5.

Contacts **Turks & Caicos Islands Tourist Board.** ✉ *Stubbs Diamond Plaza, Grace Bay, Providenciales* ☎ *649/946–4970* ⊕ *www.turksandcaicostourism.com.*

ONLINE TRAVEL TOOLS
To make the most of your vacation, check out the website for *Where-WhenHow* magazine, which has links to everything in the Turks and Caicos and an extensive dining guide. A great up-to-the minute resource for events and specials can be found on the website for *Enews;* it's updated every Wednesday. For everything you need to know about Salt Cay, there's a great little site put together by the residents there.

Contacts *Enews.* This is a great resource with a regularly updated island event calendar. ⊕ *www.TCIEnews.com.* **SaltCay.org.** This site is a good source for information about what's happening on the little island of Salt Cay. ⊕ *www.SaltCay.org.* **WhereWhenHow.** This is an excellent reference for what is going on around the islands. Their restaurant guide is also comprehensive and updated regularly. ⊕ *www.WhereWhenHow.com.*

INDEX

PHOTO CREDITS

Front cover: Chris A. Crumley / Alamy [Description: Snorkelers with sea stars, Grace Bay, Turks & Caicos]. Spine: Vilainecrevette / Shutterstock.1, Stephen Frink Collection / Alamy. 2, Jsnover | Dreamstime.com. 3 (top), Tropical Imaging. 3 (bottom), Big Blue Unlimited. 4 (top left), Ramunas Bruzas | Dreamstime. com. 4 (top right), Quinton Dean. 4 (bottom), Stephen Frink Collection / Alamy. 5 (top), Amanresorts. 5 (bottom), Aleksei Potov/ Shutterstock. 6 (top and bottom), Ramona Settle. 7, Stephen Frink Collection / Alamy. 8 (top left), idreamphoto / Shutterstock. 8 (top right), Ersler Dmitry / Shutterstock. 8 (bottom), Courtesy of Seven Stars Resort. Chapter 1: Experience the Turks and Caicos: 11, Terrance Klassen / age fotostock. Chapter 2: Providenciales: 25, BlueOrange Studio / Shutterstock. Chapter 3: The Caicos and the Cays: 101, Abbie Enock / age fotostock. Chapter 4: Grand Turk: 125, Terrance Klassen / age fotostock. Chapter 5: Salt Cay: 147, Purestock/ age fotostock.

Fodor's InFocus TURKS & CAICOS ISLANDS

Publisher: Amanda D'Acierno, *Senior Vice President*

Editorial: Arabella Bowen, *Editor in Chief*; Linda Cabasin, *Editorial Director*

Design: Tina Malaney, *Associate Art Director*; Chie Ushio, *Senior Designer*

Photography: Jennifer Arnow, *Senior Photo Editor*; Mary Robnett, *Photo Researcher*

Production: Linda Schmidt, *Managing Editor*; Evangelos Vasilakis, *Associate Managing Editor*; Angela L. McLean, *Senior Production Manager*

Maps: Rebecca Baer, *Senior Map Editor*; David Lindroth, *Cartographer*

Sales: Jacqueline Lebow, *Sales Director*

Marketing & Publicity: Heather Dalton, *Marketing Director*; Katherine Punia, *Publicity Director*

Business & Operations: Susan Livingston, *Vice President, Strategic Business Planning*; Sue Daulton, *Vice President, Operations*

Fodors.com: Megan Bell, *Executive Director, Revenue & Business Development*; Yasmin Marinaro, *Senior Director, Marketing & Partnerships*

Copyright © 2016 by Fodor's Travel, a division of Penguin Random House LLC

Writer: Laura Adzich-Brander
Editors: Perrie Hartz, Alexis Kelly
Production Editor: Carolyn Roth

3rd Edition

ISBN 978-1-101-87852-1

ISSN 1946–3049

All details in this book are based on information supplied to us at press time. Always confirm information when it matters, especially if you're making a detour to visit a specific place. Fodor's expressly disclaims any liability, loss, or risk, personal or otherwise, that is incurred as a consequence of the use of any of the contents of this book.

SPECIAL SALES

This book is available at special discounts for bulk purchases for sales promotions or premiums. For more information, e-mail specialmarkets@penguinrandomhouse.com.

PRINTED IN THE UNITED STATES OF AMERICA
10 9 8 7 6 5 4 3 2 1

ABOUT OUR WRITER

Laura Adzich-Brander was initially drawn to the Turks & Caicos Islands through her love of travel and the call of the sea. She has been a full time resident on Providenciales for over 15 years, working as a teacher and freelance writer. She has contributed cover stories and dining reviews to *WhereWhen-How,* the official guide to Providenciales and the Turks and Caicos Islands, as well as to TCI's *Times of the Island.* In addition, Laura co-authored the country's Environmental Curriculum, working as the project's Educational Consultant for The National Trust.